Mindfulness of Buddhahood in Life:
Revolutionary Insights of the Lotus Sutra

Written by
Minerva T.Y. Lee

Translator of
The Lotus Sutra and Its Opening and Closing Sutras:
A Beautiful Translation with Deep Love
from a Lay Buddhist Practitioner

Lotus Happiness | Singapore

Mindfulness of Buddhahood in Life:
Revolutionary Insights of the Lotus Sutra

Author: Minerva T. Y. Lee
Copyeditor: Keith G. and Amanda C.
Front Cover Design: Lee Theng Wei

ISBN-13: 978-981-11-6581-8

Singapore National Library Board Cataloguing-in-Publication Data is available

Published by Lotus Happiness | Singapore
http://www.lotus-happiness.com

Printed in the United States of America

For my parents,
my two baby bodhisattvas,
and YOU,
a Buddha-in-the-Making

सद्धर्मपुण्डरीकसूत्र

妙法蓮華經

དམ་ཆོས་པད་མ་དཀར་པོའི་མདོ

Table of Contents

Preface

I am eternally fortunate and grateful to have been born into a Buddhist family, which enabled me to encounter the Lotus Sutra so early in my life. Back in the 1990s in Malaysia, when I was about ten years old, I chanced upon the title of the Lotus Sutra in three Chinese characters, "Fa Hua Ying" (法华经), in one of the Chinese Dharma books. I remember vividly that particular moment when I stared in awe at the three Chinese characters and literally felt the kingly aura exuding from the title, seeping through the entire fibre of my being.

My parents practiced a syncretic mix of Taoism and Chinese Buddhism. We had a beautiful white statue of Guan Yin at home, and my mother would lead the recitation of the Great Compassion Sutra once in a very blue moon. Nevertheless, the experience of chanting the Guan Yin's mantra, "Devotion to Bodhisattva Avalokitesvara," left an indelible mark upon my consciousness. Only years later did I come to realize that Guan Yin, my beloved bodhisattva, actually appears in Chapter 25 of the Lotus Sutra.

When I was about twelve years old, I encountered the Lotus Sutra again from my maternal grandmother who taught me the daimoku: "Nam Myoho Renge Kyo." I joyously learned the mantra from her and started chanting right away. This was how I ended up practicing the Lotus Sutra through Nichiren Buddhism.

After graduating with a business degree from the National University of Singapore (NUS), and after working in the corporate world for seven years, I decided to take a leap of faith to fulfill my aspiration of becoming an author. In 2014, I successfully self-published my first book: *The Lotus Sutra and Its Opening and Closing Sutras: A Beautiful Translation with Deep Love from a Lay Buddhist Practitioner.*

One of my spiritual friends told me that I was receiving "messages" about the Buddha's teachings through "divine channelling." Call it divine channelling or psychic intuition—whatever name it is given, I believe that my intuitive understanding of the Lotus Sutra may have its origin not only through my personal efforts, but also through the karmic experiences of past lives. Age matters. Many people follow their life paths and end up discovering what they are 'meant to do' sometime between the ages of 30 and 36. For example, Shakyamuni Buddha achieved enlightenment at age 35, Lee Kuan Yew became Prime Minister of Singapore at age 35, and Daisaku Ikeda became president of Soka Gakkai at age 32. As for me, I completed my translation of the Lotus Sutra at age 31 and published my commentary on the Lotus Sutra at age 35. I believe writing about the Lotus Sutra is my personal mission, and it is predestined for the benefit of humanity.

The special affinity I share with the Lotus Sutra is inexplicable and yet deeply personal. A melting pot of predilection, purpose, and passion in my heart drives me to be an independent seeker of truth in the Buddha's teachings. While I am not a Buddhist nun or an academic scholar, that does not deter me from expressing the profound gratitude, love, and joy the Lotus Sutra inspires in me through my written works.

Every day, I am literally living and breathing the Lotus Sutra. Whenever I am walking, chanting, reading, or resting, my mind is totally absorbed in the Lotus Sutra. That enables my entire mind and my entire consciousness to be wholly in tune with the ultimate Dharma. When I read the works of the noble masters, I first absorb everything they teach in my mind. Then I allow these ideas to digest, assimilate, and sink into my sub-consciousness so that I can *feel* the teachings, not just *think* about the teachings.

I always ask myself, "How do I feel about the ideas? Do they resonate with me?" My total spiritual immersion in the Lotus Sutra gives me numerous sudden awakenings, intuitions, and insights with respect to understanding the meaning of the Lotus Sutra. In short, do not underestimate the power of single-mindedness, because it helps one to connect with the Heart of the Buddha.

Writing about the Lotus Sutra as a lay female Buddhist comes with some unexpected advantages. First, I have the complete freedom to be original in my work, free from the shackles arising from the established monastic or scholastic institution. Second, by tapping into my female intuition, I have the freedom to view things from a perspective that is different from my male Buddhist counterparts. I don't just perceive the Dharma analytically, using my head, but experience the essence and energy of the teachings in my heart. Studying the scriptures and commentaries using my heart enables me to grasp the wisdom in the Lotus Sutra in a refreshing way, and this is exactly what makes this book so special.

While I studied the works of Zhiyi and Nichiren, I experienced an inexplicable spiritual dissonance. This was exacerbated by the exclusive and elitist teachings, or rather "organizational indoctrinations," by some of the Nichiren sects. It is this spiritual disenchantment that propels me to revolutionize the philosophy of the Lotus Sutra by sharing my alternative interpretations as written in this book. When I was a beginner in Buddhism, I accepted everything the Buddhist masters said. As I grew older, and as my experiences and horizons expanded, it dawned on me that what is deemed "true" is only a subjective opinion conditioned by many external factors.

Everything I share in this book is the crystallization of five years (2014 – 2018) of intensive study and contemplation of the Lotus Sutra. In this book you will find many refreshingly original ideas and innovative perspectives that are vastly different from the interpretations of Buddhist masters such as Zhiyi and Nichiren. There may be some unorthodox insights that you may not agree with, but I encourage you to learn about the ideas with an open mind and a joyously magnanimous heart. You are free to choose what you believe is true and ditch that which you do not find relevant. I also encourage you to be a spiritual trailblazer by discovering your own insights rather than just following everything I say (or following what you have been taught by past Buddhist masters).

Through feeling the Buddha's teachings in my heart and trusting my intuition and my inner voice, I gained many creative insights in the way I approach the understanding of the Dharma. Rather than creating an entirely new doctrine—such as how Zhiyi derived his new theory of Ichinen Sanzen and Threefold Truths—I choose to understand the metaphors, images, and parables found in the Lotus Sutra just as they are. Once I have that understanding, only then do I try to find links and connections between these images and the fundamental Buddhist teachings such as the Triple Gems, the Trikaya, the Four Virtues, and so on.

All past Buddhist masters and scholars perceive the Buddha's teachings in terms of the wisdom aspect of the Buddha, namely the teaching of Buddhahood. In this book, I will show you one aspect of the Buddha that is sorely missing in the commentaries written by Zhiyi and Nichiren: the profound *compassion* of the Buddha. While the predominant focus of Buddhism in general and the Lotus Sutra in particular is about wisdom, compassion is the linchpin that defines the Buddha and his Dharma. Using scriptural evidence and personal interpretation, I will explain both 'why' and 'how' the Buddha expresses his profound compassion in the Lotus Sutra. This shows that the ultimate Dharma is not just about the *mind* (wisdom and meditation) but also the *heart* (compassion and joy).

This book is certainly not for beginners in Buddhism. Having some intermediate to advanced background in Buddhism and the Lotus Sutra will be tremendously helpful for you to appreciate the content in a more rewarding way. As you read the book, you will encounter a notation system that I established in my translation of the Lotus Sutra. As an example, the notation of "LS 21: 1.8" means "Lotus Sutra, Chapter 21, Section 1, Paragraph 8."

Happiness is the key to practicing Buddhism. I hope to share a morsel of my bliss and the wisdom of the Lotus Sutra with you so as to inspire you to embark in your personal odyssey toward the Eagle Peak of Buddhahood with peace, joy, and freedom!

Introduction

The Lotus Sutra—known as Saddharma Puṇḍarīka Sūtra in Sanskrit, Myoho Renge Kyo in Japanese, Miao Fa Lian Hua Jing in Chinese—is one of the most celebrated and influential Mahayana sutras.

As the primary Buddhist scripture in Tiantai and Nichiren Buddhism, the Lotus Sutra has enjoyed increasingly popularity among academic scholars and Nichiren Buddhist practitioners alike. Many people encounter the Lotus Sutra through Buddhist organizations such as Soka Gakkai, Nichiren Shoshu, Nichiren Shu, Rissho Kosei-Kai, and so on.

In East Asian Buddhism, most Buddhists practice the Lotus Sutra by revering Bodhisattva Avalokitesvara, also known as Guan Yin—the most renowned bodhisattva of profound loving-kindness and compassion. In Tibetan Buddhism, His Holiness the 14th Dalai Lama, Tenzin Gyatso, is considered the reincarnation of Bodhisattva Avalokitesvara. The Sanskrit mantra—Om Mani Padme Hum—means "Jewel in the Lotus." The mantra is meant to guide people to discover the jewel of Buddhahood found within the Lotus Sutra.

The Lotus Sutra is the Signature Text of Buddhism

Every religion has a single sacred text: the Bible is the holy scripture for Christianity, and so is the Qur'an for Islam and the Torah for Judaism. For traditions that do not have a single authoritative scripture, a signature text is chosen. For example, the Bhagavad-Gita is the text for Hinduism and Tao Te Ching is the scripture for Taoism.

In Buddhism, it is said that there are 84,000 sutras. As the sutras are simply too diverse, there is no single authoritative text. Different Buddhist traditions and lineages focus on different sutras. For Tendai and Nichiren Buddhism, the primary text is the Lotus Sutra. For Pure Land Buddhism, three Pure Land sutras[1] are the primary texts. For Huayan Buddhism, it is the Avatamsaka Sutra. For Vajrayana Buddhism, Prajnaparamita and tantric-related sutras are the primary texts. As Professor Donald S. Lopez, Jr., Distinguished Professor of Buddhist and Tibetan Studies at the University of Michigan, put it: "There are thousands of texts that are considered canonical by one or another of the Buddhist traditions of Asia. But if I had to choose one sutra, it would be *The Lotus Sutra*."[2]

Declared by the Buddha as the King of All Sutras, the Lotus Sutra is considered the *tour de force* of Shakyamuni Buddha's lifetime of teachings. The main reason is because the Lotus Sutra teaches the ultimate truth that everyone has the capacity to achieve Supreme Perfect Enlightenment, and quickly at that. Thus, the Lotus Sutra has become the signature text of Buddhism for many millions of people.

Is the Lotus Sutra the Word of the Buddha?

The Lotus Sutra is replete with fantastical parables, stories, metaphors. For some people, reading the Lotus Sutra is like entering an enchanting world of magic and fairytales.

Modern scholarship does not support the claim, however, that the Lotus Sutra and other Mahayana Sutras are the "Buddha's words." Nevertheless, I share the same intuition with Ajahn Sujato in regard to the sutras being written by monks who actually remembered their past life experiences during intensive meditation experiences:

"Why were the Mahayana Sutras phrased as if spoken literally by the Buddha? This is a difficult question, and there is unlikely to be one answer. Partly it was just how the literary form evolved. But I suspect, given the visionary nature of many Mahayanist texts, that they often stemmed from meditation experiences; visions of the Buddha, memories of 'teachings' received while in samadhi. Perhaps the authors of these texts believed that the Buddha was really present to them in some sense—and this is indeed the theme of many Mahayana sutras. Or perhaps they more humbly believed that they had gained insight into the Dhamma in some direct way." [3]

The fact that the Lotus Sutra can be preserved, translated, and passed down through centuries of social turbulence and political turmoil is a miracle. The discovery of original Sanskrit manuscripts in a wooden box inside a Buddhist stupa in Gilgit (now Kashmir in Pakistan) in 1931 is a veritable testament of this miracle. [4] The manuscripts of the Lotus Sutra were remarkably well-preserved, and they did not decay for several crucial reasons: first, the near-zero temperatures of the region protected the materials; and second, the manuscripts were written on the bark of the Bhoj (birch) tree, which is very durable and largely insusceptible to decay.

There is a reason why the entire sutra was so well-preserved for the future generations. In the past, most people did not have easy access to written sutras, so they were precious and cared for diligently. Now, we are exceptionally fortunate, because we can readily find and read the Lotus Sutra in dozens of different languages via books or the Internet. Whenever I think of how the Lotus Sutra was painstakingly kept and preserved, I am awed by the destiny and mission of the Lotus Sutra to benefit generations of humanity.

In the Mahaparinirvana Sutra, the Buddha cautioned his disciples "to follow the teachings, not men; the meaning, not the word; true wisdom, not shallow understanding."[5] Therefore, whether the Lotus Sutra or any Mahayana sutras were literally 'spoken' by the Buddha is beside the point. The ultimate Dharma is beyond words. We need to look beyond the superficial meaning of words by reading between the lines and understanding their intricate meanings to grasp the essence of the Buddha's teachings.

The Wisdom of the Lotus Sutra is Buddhahood

Many perceive the Buddha-Dharma as the Four Noble Truths, the Eightfold Path, and the Twelve-linked Chains of Causation. Some people even think that Buddhism is all about mindfulness and meditation. The truth is: attaining Buddhahood to completely uproot and be liberated from all sufferings is ultimate purpose of the Buddha's teachings.

The Lotus Sutra is the embodiment of the Dharmakaya of the Eternal Buddha who transcends the conventional concepts with respect to the name and form of a particular Buddha. This means that the Eternal Buddha, the Transcendental Buddha, or the Original Buddha does not have a specific name such as Shakyamuni Buddha, Amitabha Buddha, Mahavairocana Buddha, Bodhisattva Samantabhadra, or even Nichiren. In fact, the Eternal Buddha dwells within *you*.

The teaching of Buddhahood is taught across all traditions of Buddhism. In Theravada Buddhism, one is taught to attain Nibbana,[6] or the state of birthlessness and deathlessness, as the goal of the practice. In Tibetan Buddhism, we are taught to have bodhicitta, which means the altruistic wish to attain enlightenment for the sake of all sentient beings. In Pure Land Buddhism, practitioners aspire to be reborn in the pure land of Amitabha to continue the practice toward Buddhahood. In Zen Buddhism, disciples of the Zen Master are taught to experience sudden enlightenment through a koan or by performing the most mundane tasks throughout their daily lives. In Nichiren Buddhism, disciples are taught to chant the daimoku of "Nam Myoho Renge Kyo" to awaken their innate Buddhahood.

Every sutra has its own nature. Just as the Metta Sutta is about loving kindness, the Prajnaparamita Sutra is about emptiness, and the Satipatthana Sutta is about mindfulness, the Lotus Sutra is about Supreme Perfect Enlightenment, or Buddhahood. In other words, the Lotus Sutra is a teaching of 'the ultimate' Dharma. While other Mahayana sutras such as the Amitabha Sutra, Heart Sutra, and Diamond Sutra mention *Anuttara Samyak Sambodhi* (Sanskrit for Supreme Perfect Enlightenment, or Buddhahood), it is the Lotus Sutra that specifically focuses on describing the 'what' of *Anuttara Samyak Sambodhi* and the 'how' to achieve Buddhahood quickly.

The wisdom of the Lotus Sutra is Buddhahood. In the Lotus Sutra, the Law of Buddhahood is expressed as the *One Buddha-Vehicle* (一佛乘). Terms related to Buddhahood include:

- Ekayana / One Vehicle (一乘)
- Buddhayana /Buddha Vehicle (佛乘)
- Dharmadhatu / Dharma Realm (法界)
- Tathagatagarbha (如来藏)
- Buddha-nature (佛性)
- Suchness (真如)
- Dharmakaya / Dharma Body (法身)
- Great Nirvana[6] (大涅槃)

- Birthless and Deathless（不生不灭）
- Anuttara Samyak Sambodhi (阿耨多罗三藐三菩提)

The Sanskrit term *Anuttara Samyak Sambodhi* is the keyword that appears in most Mahayana sutras. Let us see how many times this keyword appears in some of the most popular Mahayana sutras:

Name of Mahayana Sutra	No. of Times
Lotus Sutra	89
Heart Sutra	1
Diamond Sutra	29
Amitabha Sutra	4
Vimalakirti Sutra	44

Table 1: Number of Times Anuttara Samyak Sambodhi Appears in the Sutras

Here are some scriptural examples of the presence of the keyword *Anuttara Samyak Sambodhi* in Mahayana sutras and the Pali Canon:

#1 – Heart Sutra

> *"By way of prajna paramita, Buddhas of the past, present, and future attain **Anuttara Samyak Sambodhi**."*[7]

#2 – Diamond Sutra

> *"Subhuti, in the **Anuttara Samyak Sambodhi**, all dharmas thusly should be known, thus be viewed, and thus be sincerely understood as the unborn appearances of dharmas. Subhuti, the words 'dharma appearances,' the Tathagata has said, then, are not dharma appearances. This is called dharma appearances."*[8]

#3 – Amitabha Sutra

"Sariputra, if there are people who have already made the vow, who now make the vow, or who are about to make the vow, 'I desire to be born in Amitabha's Country', these people, whether born in the past, now being born, or to be born in the future, all will irreversibly attain **Anuttara Samyak Sambodhi.** *Therefore, Sariputra, all good men and good women, if they are among those who have faith, should make the vow, 'I will be born in that country.'"⁹*

#4 – Vimalakirti Sutra

"Good people, if you wish to gain the Buddha body and do away with the ills that afflict all living beings, then you must set your minds on attaining **Anuttara Samyak Sambodhi.** *"¹⁰*

#5 – Turning the Dharma Wheel:

"Bhikṣus, in regard to these three turnings and twelve motions of the Four Noble Truths, if they had not given birth to vision, wisdom, understanding, and Bodhi, then amongst all the devas, māras, brahmās, śramaṇas, and brāhmaṇas who hear the Dharma, I could not have achieved liberation, gone beyond, and departed. I also would not have had self-realization of the attainment of **Anuttara Samyak Sambodhi.** *Yet I have, from the three turnings and twelve motions of the Four Noble Truths, given birth to vision, wisdom, understanding, and Bodhi. Amongst the devas, māras, brahmās, śramaṇas, and brāhmaṇas who hear the Dharma, I have gone beyond and achieved liberation, and have had self-realization of the attainment of* **Anuttara Samyak Sambodhi.** *"¹¹*

The Dharma of Buddhahood Is the First and Foremost

What makes the Lotus Sutra so distinctively outstanding is its focus on the Dharma of Buddhahood. The Lotus Sutra is the crystallization of Shakyamuni Buddha's lifetime of teachings, for it reveals the Dharma of the One Buddha-Vehicle to awaken the Buddha-nature of all living beings toward the pinnacle state of Buddhahood. Hence, it is not surprising that the Buddha praised the Lotus Sutra as "the first and foremost" and "the King of all Sutras." The Lotus Sutra is the champion and the *crème de la crème* of all the Buddha's teachings. Here are a few scriptural examples:

The Lotus Sutra Is the First and Foremost

> *"O Medicine King! Now I shall declare this to you:*
> *'Among the various sutras*
> *that I have expounded,*
> *the Lotus Sutra is the first and foremost!'"*
> *(LS 10: 1.20)[12]*

The Lotus Sutra Is the Crowning Glory

> *"O Manjushri! The Lotus Sutra is the foremost teaching among all sutras expounded by Tathagata. Among all sutras that I have expounded, the Lotus Sutra is the most profound. Therefore, the sutra is bestowed the last; just as the great king who at last gave away his precious bright pearl that he had guarded for so long." (LS 14: 6.9)*

The Lotus Sutra Is the King of All Sutras

> *"Among all shravakas and pratyekabuddhas, bodhisattvas are the foremost. So is the Lotus Sutra; among all sutras, it is the* **foremost!** *Just as the Buddha is the King of the Law, so is the Lotus Sutra; it is the King of all Sutras!" (LS 23: 2.8)*

White Lotus as the Metaphor for Buddhahood

The full title of the Lotus Sutra in Sanskrit—*Saddharma Pundarika Sutra*—means the "The Scripture of Magnificent Law of White Lotus." The lotus is the mother of enlightenment, for it is a Great Cause that enables each of us to become a Buddha. Among all the sutras, only the Lotus Sutra uses the white lotus as the metaphor to denote the Law of Buddhahood.

The lotus is an aquatic plant that thrives in muddy water. The lotus flower blooms and seeds at the same time. Under favorable conditions, the lotus seeds can remain viable for a long time. All parts of the lotus—flower, rhizome, seed, stem, leaves—are edible, and some of them can be used for medicinal purposes in traditional medicine.

In Buddhist iconography, the Buddhas and bodhisattvas are often depicted sitting in a lotus position on the lotus flower. Some bodhisattvas are also portrayed as holding a lotus flower. In fact, the Buddhas are documented to be "born through transformation from the lotus."[13] Thus, it is not surprising that the lotus image is the most frequently-used logo by many Buddhist organizations.

The image of the lotus, when drawn with the eight petals, resembles either a lotus flower, a sun, or a lion's mane. A lion is a metaphor for the Buddha, and the lion's roar means "the Buddha's teachings." Nichiren, which means "Sun Lotus," is his chosen Dharma name.

The lotus, being white in color, symbolises the truth of purity. White can also denote the doctrine of Emptiness, a doctrine that is widely expounded in the Perfection of Wisdom sutra (Prajnaparamita Sutra). Nichiren Buddhism teaches the doctrine of "simultaneity of the Law of Cause and Effect" because the lotus blooms and seeds at the same time.

Meaning of Lotus through the Chinese Characters

Chinese characters are beautiful because multiple meanings can be inferred through the form and sound of the characters. The Lotus Sutra in Chinese is "Miao Fa Lian Hua Jing" (妙法莲华经). Now, let us understand the meaning the Lotus Sutra from the Chinese title.

Wonderful Dharma - Miao Fa (妙法)

The character "miao" is a word of praise because it means wonderful, exquisite, splendid, marvellous, and magnificent. Alternatively, it can also mean special, unique, or distinctive. In Soka Gakkai, Miao Fa (妙法) is translated as the "Mystic Law." The adjective "mystic" means cryptic, esoteric, secret, occult, or mysterious, which is not aligned with "miao" as a word to praise the Dharma.

The character "fa" means the Buddha-Dharma, Law, phenomena, reality, way, or method. It is interesting to note that this Chinese character is composed of two separate characters that mean "water" and "remove," respectively. Thus, it symbolizes that the Dharma is like water, capable of cleansing the impurities in life.

The two characters "Miao Fa" can also mean "special method." In Tibetan Buddhism, the way to attaining Buddhahood is a gradual, step-by-step method that is anchored upon guru devotion and some secret tantric practices. On the contrary, the Lotus Sutra is the "special method" to practice the way of Buddhahood through the profound wisdom and compassion of the Buddha by means of a sutra.

Lotus - Lian Hua (莲华)

The Chinese word "lian" (莲) means lotus. Homophonically speaking, however, "lian" has multiple meanings. First, the phonetic sound of "lian" is similar to another Chinese word "lian" (连) that means "connect." The character "che" (车) inside the character "lian" means "car," i.e., a transport vehicle. Thus, the character "lian" denotes not only the lotus but also possesses the hidden meanings of "connection" and "vehicle."

The Law of Buddhahood in the Lotus Sutra is expressly referred to as the One Buddha Vehicle (一佛乘). This means that the Law of Lotus is a type of "vehicle" that transports a person from the ocean of suffering to the shore of enlightenment.

Another meaning of "lian" is connection or relationship. One of the methods to attain Buddhahood is by associating with good friends—a testament to the importance of kinship, friendship, and personal network.

The Chinese word "hua" (华 means flower. Lovely and beautiful, a flower has many implicit meanings associated with it, such as achievement, success, and abundance. In many civilizations and cultures, flowers are an expression of honour, praise, and beauty. By giving flowers, we honour and recognise the glorious achievement of a person.

The character "hua" (化) that is within "hua" (华) means "transformation." This indicates that life at the realm of Buddhahood is born not through egg, womb, or moisture[14] but is that of transformation through a lotus flower, which means transformation by means of the Dharma.

Put together, the characters "lian hua" denote "Connecting Abundance" or "Success through Relationship." In other words, the lotus has the hidden meaning of "attaining Buddhahood through associating with Dharma friends or teachers."

The Essence of the Lotus Sutra Is Compassion

Most, if not all past and present Buddhist masters perceived the Lotus Sutra as the ultimate teaching of the Buddha because it is a teaching that enables people to rapidly attain Buddhahood. However, not many people view the Lotus Sutra as the quintessence of compassion.

It was a moment of indescribable awakening when I suddenly perceived the Lotus Sutra as the ultimate expression of the Buddha's profound compassion. In the past, when I thought about the Lotus Sutra, the only keyword that came to my mind was "Buddhahood." Now, the keyword is "compassion."

The essence of a Buddha is compassion. And compassion is expressed in unconditional generosity. Without the generous giving by the Buddha, attaining Buddhahood would have been a Sisyphean task for most people. Practicing Buddhism, in its very essence, is the cultivation of generosity and compassion in our thoughts, speech, and actions.

In this book, I will show you not only the wisdom, but also the compassion of the Lotus Sutra—an aspect that is seldom analysed in the commentaries written by most Buddhist masters. You will discover how the Buddha manifests his profound compassion by doling out the "Three Gifts" of Law, Life, and Love to his disciples, which will be amply explained in Section 1: Insights of the Lotus Sutra.

Section 1:

The Three Gifts

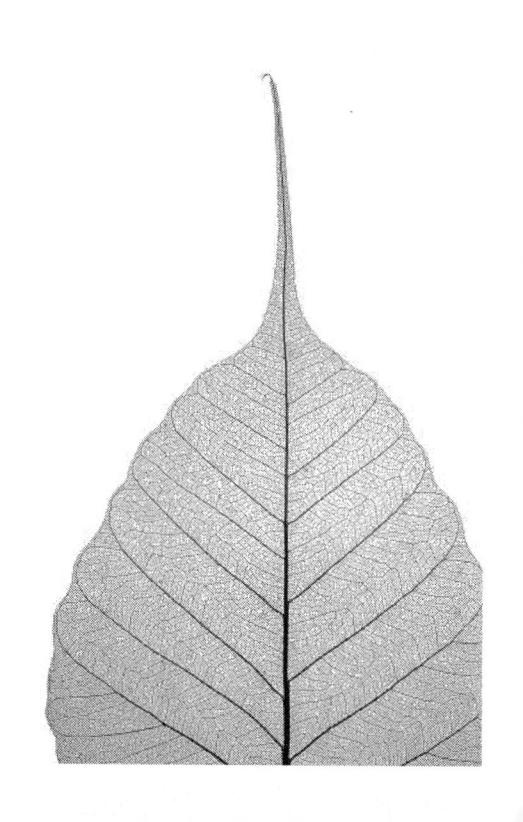

Insights of Past Buddhist Masters

Dao Sheng

Dao Sheng (道生) (ca 364 – 434) was a Chinese Buddhist scholar known for promulgating the concepts of sudden enlightenment and the universality of the Buddha-nature. He wrote a book entitled *Commentary on the Lotus Sutra.*[1]

He understood the lotus flower as having both fruit and blossoms, which symbolize the simultaneity of cause and effect. He also concluded that the Lotus Sutra is the Dharma of wonderful cause and wonderful effect, which results in his segregation of the Lotus Sutra into two halves based on the principle of cause and effect.[2]

Zhiyi / Chih-I

Zhiyi or Chih-I (智顗) (538 –597 CE), the fourth patriarch in his lineage, is generally considered the founder of Tiantai Buddhism (Jp. Tendai) in China. Tiantai Buddhism is an esoteric Buddhism that reveres the Lotus Sutra as Shakyamuni Buddha's ultimate teachings. It is also an eclectic style of Buddhism because multiple practices ranging from meditations, devotional practices, and esoteric rituals using mudras, mantras, and visualizations are included in the Zhiyi's teachings.

Zhiyi is the first person to break away from the Indian tradition to establish an indigenous Chinese system. He is also credited with the classification of the sutras into a meaningful system. His three major works are:

- *Great Concentration and Insight* (摩诃止观 Mohe Zhiguan)
- *Words and Phrases of the Lotus Sutra* (法華文句 Fahua Wenju)
- *Profound Meaning of the Lotus Sutra* (法華玄義 Fahua Xuanyi).

His three major philosophies of the Lotus Sutra are:
- The Five Periods and Eight Teachings (五時八教 Wu Shi Ba Jiao)
- Three Thousand Realms in a Single Moment of Life (一念三千 Yi Nian San Qian)
- Threefold Truths (圓融三谛 Yuan Rong San Di).

While Zhiyi declared that the Lotus Sutra is a teaching that "Exposes the Expedient and Reveals the Truth" (开权显实) and identified the Lotus Sutra as the complete doctrine in his "The Five Periods and Eight Teachings," most of his philosophies are not entirely related to the Lotus Sutra, resulting in the many "offshoot" Buddhist sects that do not focus on the Lotus Sutra as the core teaching.

For instance, when Tiantai Buddhism was imported to Japan by Saicho, different Buddhist monks who studied Tendai Buddhism went on to establish different Buddhist sects by choosing different aspects of Zhiyi's teaching. Dogen focused on Zhiyi's meditation practices and founded Soto Zen Buddhism (although he quoted the Lotus Sutra far more than any other sutras)[3], Honen focused on the Amitabha Buddha's teaching as taught by Zhiyi and founded Pure Land Buddhism, and Nichiren focused on the Lotus Sutra and founded Nichiren Buddhism, which anchors upon the chanting of the daimoku (the title of the Lotus Sutra) as the core practice.

Nichiren

Nichiren （ 日 蓮 ） (1222 – 1281) was the 13th-century Japanese Buddhist reformist who was known for his unshakable devotion to the Lotus Sutra. He advocated the chanting of the daimoku, Nam Myoho Renge Kyo, as the core practice for people living in the Dharma-declining age (Latter Day of the Law). The daimoku is an innovative practice established by Nichiren to awaken and polish the Buddhahood within us.

The works of Nichiren include the *Gosho* (compilation of letters to his disciples) and the *Record of the Orally Transmitted Teachings*. Disciples of Nichiren Buddhism study the *Gosho* to receive guidance from the perspectives and interpretations of Nichiren with respect to the practice of the Lotus Sutra.

Nichiren is known for his strong personality and his uncompromising attitude toward other Buddhist sects and philosophies. Thus, many followers of Nichiren Buddhism are somewhat influenced by his exclusivist stance with respect to the understanding of non-Nichiren Buddhist schools and doctrines.

Overview of My Insights

I believe that each interpretation of the Lotus Sutra is significantly influenced by an individual's idiosyncratic personality, disposition, temperament, aspirations, life experiences, and intellectual capacity. However, the cultural, socio-economic, and political conditions in a country during a specific era also play a critical role in shaping the philosophical slants of the Buddhist masters with respect to understanding the Lotus Sutra.

All the insights of the Lotus Sutra presented in this book are, to a great extent, a reflection of who I am. The inspirations, ideas, and insights came to me in bits and pieces over the span of five years. To facilitate readers' understanding of my insights, I include an overview of the structures of my insights.

Essentially, I have categorized the understanding of the Lotus Sutra in two parts: Theoretical and Scriptural Understanding, and Practices and Applications.

#1 - Theoretical and Scriptural Understanding of the Lotus Sutra

- The Three Gifts (Compassion)
    - Law
    - Life
    - Love
- Buddha in the Sky (Wisdom)
    - Emptiness
    - Middle Way
    - Buddhahood

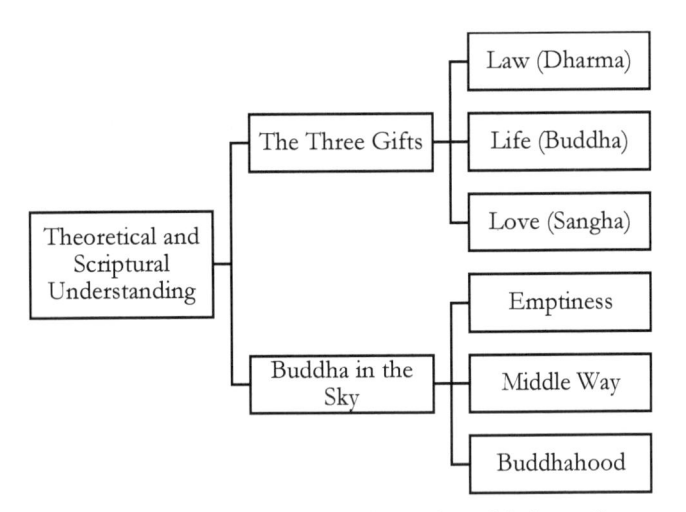

Figure 1: Theoretical and Scriptural Understanding of the Lotus Sutra

#2 - Practices and Applications of the Lotus Sutra

- The Three One-Heart Methods (Individual Practice)
  - Practice
  - Propagation
  - Mindfulness
- The Three E's of Enlightenment (Group Practice)
  - Education
  - Empowerment
  - Engagement
    - Music
    - Meditation
    - Movement
    - Mandala

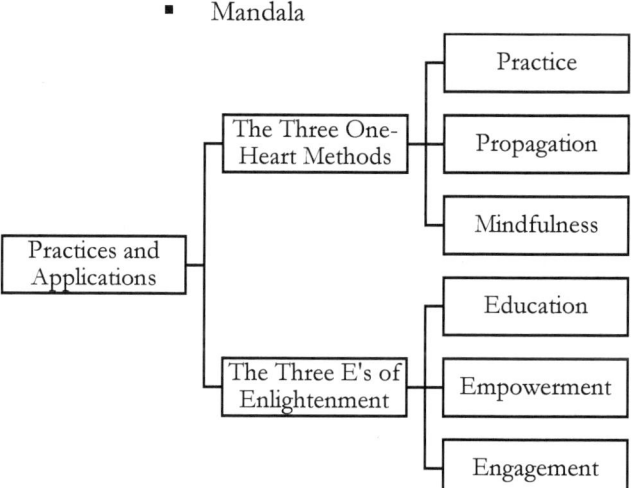

Figure 2: Practices and Applications of the Lotus Sutra

In brief, the two parts of Theoretical and Scriptural Understanding, as well as Practices and Applications, provide a big-picture overview of my insights of the Lotus Sutra.

Overall Framework in Terms of the Four Virtues

Let me share with you a big-picture framework in terms of Four Virtues to summarize all my innovative ideas and theories in this book:

True Self	Eternity
Three Gifts (Compassion)	Buddha in the Sky (Wisdom)
<ul><li>Gift of Law</li><li>Gift of Life</li><li>Gift of Love</li></ul>	<ul><li>The Law of Emptiness</li><li>The Law of Middle Way</li><li>The Law of Buddhahood</li></ul>
Purity	**Happiness**
Three One-Heart Methods (Individual Practice):	Three E's of Enlightenment (Group Practice):
<ul><li>Practice</li><li>Propagation</li><li>Mindfulness</li></ul>	<ul><li>Education</li><li>Empowerment</li><li>Engagement</li></ul>

Figure 3: Big-Picture Framework in Terms of Four Virtues

The *True Self* of a Buddha means not only the Dharmakaya of the Eternal Buddha, but also the quality of profound compassion. *Eternity* means the wisdom of the Dharma that is unchanging, adamantine, and everlasting. *Purity* means the Dharma practice that enables us to purify our lives. And lastly, *Happiness* means the joy and bliss of practicing the Dharma in a community of Sangha that celebrates diversity and inclusiveness.

Structure of the Lotus Sutra

All Buddhist masters perceive the structure of the Lotus Sutra differently. The following are the structures as understood by three Buddhist teachers: Dao Sheng, Zhiyi (and Nichiren), and Thich Nhat Hanh.

#1 - Dao Sheng

Dao Sheng understood the structure of the Lotus Sutra in terms of the Law of Cause and Effect on the One Vehicle:[4]

Chapters	Interpretations
Chapters 1–14	Cause of the Three Vehicles is the cause of the One Vehicle.
Chapters 15–21	Effect of the Three Vehicles is the effect of the One Vehicle
Chapters 22–28	The practitioners of the Three Vehicles are the practitioners of the One Vehicle

Table 2: Structure of the Lotus Sutra by Dao Sheng

#2 – Zhiyi (and Nichiren)

According to Zhiyi, the Lotus Sutra is segmented into two major parts: expedient/provisional teachings (Chapters 1 – 14) and essential teachings (Chapters 15 – 28).[5] Besides, Zhiyi taught that Chapters 2 and 16 are the key chapters of the Lotus Sutra. Nichiren adopted the teaching of Zhiyi, and hence, it is not surprising that most Nichiren Buddhists recite parts of Chapters 2 and 16 in their daily rituals.

Chapters	Interpretations
Chapters 1–14:	Expedient/Provisional Teachings (Chapter 2 is key chapter)
Chapters 15–28:	Essential Teachings (Chapter 16 is key chapter)

Table 3: Structure of the Lotus Sutra by Zhiyi and Nichiren

#2 – Thich Nhat Hanh

On the other hand, Thich Nhat Hanh segregates the Lotus Sutra into three parts: the historical dimension, the ultimate dimension, and the action dimension.[6]

Chapters	Interpretations
Chapters 1–14:	Historical Dimension
Chapters 15–21:	Ultimate Dimension
Chapters 22–28:	Action Dimension

Table 4: Structure of the Lotus Sutra by Thich Nhat Hanh

My Structure of the Lotus Sutra

I perceive the structure Lotus Sutra in terms of the Triple Gems of Buddha, Dharma, and Sangha. These Triple Gems can also be understood as The Three Gifts of Law, Life, and Love, which I will explain in detail later.

Taking refuge in the Triple Gems is the fundamental practice of Buddhists in most traditions. Most, if not all, people think that embracing the Lotus Sutra does not entail taking the Triple Refuge. This is not true at all. The structure of the Lotus Sutra in terms of the Triple Gems is the proof that the Triple Refuge is already embedded within the Lotus Sutra. As such, embracing the Lotus Sutra is tantamount to taking refuge in the Triple Gems.

The diagram below is the overall structure in terms of the Triple Gems and the Three Gifts of Law, Life, and Love:

Chapters	Three Gifts	Triple Gems	Teachings
1–16	Law	Dharma	The One Buddha-Vehicle is the Bodhi seed
11–22	Life	Buddha	Transmission of the merits of Dharmakaya of an Eternal Buddha to the disciples
23–28	Love	Sangha	Compassionate actions of bodhisattvas as exemplary role models

Table 5: My Structure of the Lotus Sutra

The Three Gifts and the Triple Refuge

Among all the sutras, only the Lotus Sutra is repeatedly declared by the Buddha as the first and foremost (LS 10: 1.20, LS 11: 3.35, LS 20: 2.12) and the King of All Sutras (LS 23: 2.6, LS 23: 2.8, LS 10:2.17). From my personal contemplation and insights, there are three primary reasons why the Lotus Sutra is eminently unrivalled:

- Gift of the Law (Dharma)
- Gift of Life (Buddha)
- Gift of Love (Sangha)

The Gift of the Law is the aspect of *Dharma* that embodies the Buddha's wisdom. The Gift of Life is the aspect of *Buddha* that reveals the Dharmakaya of an Eternal Buddha. The Gift of Love is the aspect of *Sangha* that focuses on compassion as the core practice.

The letter L means Lotus, Life, Love, Law, Lead, Learn, Legacy, etc. To make the Three Gifts easy to remember by connecting them with the L of lotus, I name them with words that begin with L— Law, Life, and Love. Nevertheless, I am perfectly aware of the imperfections in terms of connotations of these words. For example, the Sanskrit word *Dharma* is a far better word than the English word *Law* because the word *Law* has such unsavory associations with courts, justice, and punishment. Thus, the term "Mystic Law" does not capture the beauty of the Buddha's teachings as much as the term "Wonderful Dharma." As for the word *Love*, it has the negative connotations of desire, lust, and attachment. In spite of that, using the three words Law, Life, and Love is an application of alliteration (words that start with the same consonant sound), a type of poetic device that makes the Three Gifts splendidly poetic.

1 - *Gift of the Law (Dharma)*
The One Buddha-Vehicle is the Seed of Buddhahood

Theoretically speaking, the revelation of the One Buddha-Vehicle is the essence of the Lotus Sutra because it teaches the universal enlightenment of all sentient beings. The most wonderful aspect of the Lotus Sutra, however, is the delineation of the One Buddha-Vehicle as the Gift of the Law through the Seven Parables.

As I studied the Lotus Sutra, I noticed that the Chinese character "Yi" (一), which means number one, kept appearing in the text. The number one symbolizes the leader, the king, and the champion. The presence of the number one denotes that the Lotus Sutra is truly the *crème de la crème* of the ultimate Dharma.

There are six different types of "One" as found in the Lotus Sutra. For the purpose of explaining the Gift of the Law, I will explain only the One Buddha-Vehicle in this section.

1. One Buddha-Vehicle (一佛乘)
2. All (一切)
3. First and Foremost (第一)
4. One Heart (一心)
5. One Buddha-Land (一佛土)
6. One Mindfulness (一念)

The term "vehicle" means that the Buddha's teaching functions like a ship capable of transporting a person from the ocean of suffering to the shore of enlightenment. The term is a metaphoric way of expressing the purpose of the Buddha's teachings in eliminating suffering of the people by leading them to enlightenment.

Understand the One Buddha-Vehicle in the Context of the Expedient Methods

> *"Only the Law of One-Vehicle*
> *exists in the Buddha-lands everywhere in the ten directions;*
> *there is no second or third Vehicle,*
> *unless the Buddha expounds via expedient methods." (LS 2:*
> *5.16)[7]*

The meaning of One Buddha-Vehicle is derived by understanding the term "Expedient Methods," because the Buddha revealed the One Buddha-Vehicle in the context of the Expedient Methods in Chapter 2.

All pre- and post-Lotus Sutra teachings are considered dharma of the expedient methods because the focus of the Buddha's discourses ranges across morality, meditation, emptiness, suffering, and impermanence rather than the goal of Buddhahood.

In this sense, the Buddha is like a "situational leader" who is firm in his goal but flexible in his approach. He understands that every individual is different, which means that there is no one-size-fits-all approach and solution. Therefore, he teaches wisely in a contextualized manner to tailor to the natures, desires, and intellectual capacity of his disciples. This method of customizing and contextualizing his teachings according to circumstances is what we mean by Expedient Methods or Skillful Means.

The One Buddha-Vehicle—Not the Ten Factors—Is the Essence

Chapter 2 can be segmented into two parts: the "provisional" part, in which the 5,000 disciples remained in the assembly, and the "essential" part, in which the 5,000 disciples departed the assembly. Zhiyi perceived the Ten Factors as the "essence" of the Buddha's teachings, and he used the Ten Factors to derive his equation of Ichinen Sanzen.

The essence of Chapter 2 is not the Ten Factors, however; it is the One Buddha-Vehicle, which was expounded by the Buddha after the 5,000 disciples had left the assembly.

The term "One Buddha-Vehicle" is the key word of the Lotus Sutra, and it means "Anuttara Samyaka Sambodhi" or Buddhahood. In Chapter 2, the Buddha revealed and repeated the same term seven times (LS 2: 4.7, 4.8, 4.9, 4.10, 4.11, 4.12, 4.15),[8] but I will show only three as examples:

> *The Buddha said to Shariputra: "The Buddhas-Tathagatas only teach and transform bodhisattvas. All that they do is for one purpose—that is to show and awaken all living beings to the Buddha-wisdom. O Shariputra! The Tathagatas teach all living beings only by means of the* **One Buddha-Vehicle;** *there is no alternative Vehicle, neither the second nor the third. O Shariputra! The teachings of the Buddhas in the ten directions are identical." (LS 2: 4.7)*

> *"O Shariputra! All present Buddhas-Bhagavats, dwelling in immeasurable hundreds of thousands of millions of billions of Buddha-lands in the ten directions, bestow an abundance of benefits, blessings, peace, and joy to living beings. The Buddhas also apply immeasurable expedient methods—causes and conditions, metaphors, similes, parables, and various linguistic expressions—to expound the various doctrines to living beings. Because all these doctrines are derived from the* **One Buddha-Vehicle,** *living beings, having listened to the doctrines of the Buddha, will eventually attain the perfect wisdom." (LS 2: 4.10)*

> *"O Shariputra! The Buddhas appear in the evil worlds of five defilements, namely the defilement of kalpa, the defilement of suffering, the defilement of living beings, the defilement of views, and the defilement of lifespan. O Shariputra! In the age of*

chaotic kalpa, the impurities run deep. Living beings—being stingy, greedy, and envious—will not be planting virtuous roots. Therefore, all Buddhas, by applying the power of expedient methods, make differentiations to the **One Buddha-Vehicle** *by teaching it as though there are three different Vehicles." (LS 2: 4.12)*

Seven Parables to Illustrate the Gift of the Law

From the spiritual perspective, the number seven is a symbol of completion and perfection. We have seven days in a week, seven chakras in our bodies, seven colours in a rainbow, seven continents, and the list goes on. The Buddha is said to have walked seven times immediately after his birth. The Seven Parables also remind us of the Seven Factors of Enlightenment—Mindfulness, Investigation, Energy, Joy, Relaxation, Concentration, and Equanimity—that become a powerful medicine for both Mahakashyapa and Shakyamuni Buddha in times of grave illness.[9]

The number seven is equally mystifying in the Threefold Lotus Sutra. Here are some of the scriptural evidences:

- Seven-jewelled pagoda of the Abundant Treasures Buddha (LS 15: 1.6)
- Seven-jewelled lotus flower (LS 24: 1.12)
- Seven-jewelled Bodhi tree (LS 27:1.11)
- Seven-jewelled crown (LS 28: 1.13)
- Three Thousand Major Thousandfold Worlds of the Seven Treasures (LS 23:1.13)
- The Buddha's son, Rahula, is predicted to become a Buddha named Walking on Flowers of Seven Treasures Tathagata (LS 9: 3.1).
- Bodhisattva Universal Worthy's six-tusked white elephant is supported by seven legs, under which seven lotus flowers blossom (MBUW 1.10).

The One Buddha-Vehicle as the Gift of the Law is illustrated by means of the Seven Parables. The Seven Parables are akin to the science of light refraction, wherein a ray of light passes through a prism to give off the seven rainbow colors. The incoming ray of white light represents the One Buddha-Vehicle (Law of Buddhahood), the prism represents the Threefold World, and the seven colors represent the Seven Parables. Through the Seven Parables, you will gain a more concrete understanding of the meaning of One Buddha-Vehicle as the Gift of the Law.

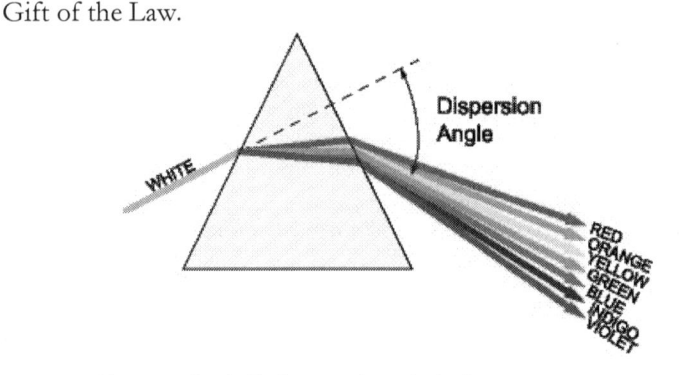

Figure 4: Light Refraction through the Prism

One Buddha-Vehicle is the Gift of the Law because the Buddha literally gives away his most guarded precious jewel to his disciples who are ready to inherit his ultimate treasure, just like a generous Santa Claus. Through the parables, you will understand three key points: first, who is the Buddha; second, the Buddha's expedient methods; third, the gift of the Buddha. The detailed stories of the Seven Parables can be found under *Appendix 7: Seven Parables of the Lotus Sutra.*

Seven Parables	The Buddha's Gift of the Law
1. Parable of a Blazing House (Chapter 3)	The Buddha is the father who promised his children three carriages (goat, deer, and ox) as the gifts if they escaped from the burning house. After the children were safely out of the burning house, he gave away his

		ultimate gift: the great white ox carriage. The Expedient Method: Promise of the three carriages outside the burning house. The Gift: Great white ox carriage.
2.	Parable of the Father and His Lost Son (Chapter 4)	The Buddha is the father who found his long-lost son suffering from an inferiority complex and low self-esteem. Eventually, the father bequeathed all his treasures to his son. The Expedient Method: The menial job for his son. The Gift: Treasures.
3.	Parable of the Medicinal Herbs (Chapter 5)	The Buddha is the great cloud which poured down the Dharma rain equally to all trees and plants. The Expedient Method: Equal pouring of rain water. The Gift: Rain water.
4.	Parable of the Imaginary City (Chapter 7)	The Buddha is the caravan leader who knew the way to reach the treasure destination. When his group members were exhausted, he magically conjured a phantom city for them to recharge so that they had the energy to reach the treasure land.

		The Expedient Method: Conjuring the phantom city. The Gifts: Wisdom, divine powers and leadership.
5.	Parable of the Jewel in the Robe (Chapter 8)	The Buddha is a good friend who secretly gave his poor friend a jewel by sewing it in the friend's robe. The Expedient Method: Giving the jewel to his poor friend in secret. The Gift: Jewel.
6.	Parable of the Precious Pearl in the Topknot (Chapter 14)	The Buddha is the king who gave away his most precious pearl in his topknot after his soldiers had proven their capabilities in the battle against devils. The Expedient Method: Giving all types of gifts. The Gift: Pearl.
7.	Parable of the Skillful Doctor (Chapter 16)	The Buddha is the father who healed his sons from the poisons by concocting the most outstanding medicines. For those who refused to take the medicines, the father resorted to a skillful means so that his most obstinate children took the medicines. The Expedient Method: Declaring his demise. The Gifts: Wisdom and medicine.

Table 6: Seven Parables to Illustrate the Gift of the Law

In sum, through the use of Seven Parables, the Buddha explains the One Buddha-Vehicle as the Gift of the Law in a vividly beautiful and effectively skillful manner.

One Buddha-Vehicle is the Seed of Buddhahood

The significance of the One Buddha-Vehicle lies in the fact that it is the seed of Buddhahood. Just as a rich field without the presence of the right seed will not result in the fruition of the right plant, the presence of Buddha-nature (fertile soil or potentiality for Buddhahood) will not result in Buddhahood if there is no teaching of the One Buddha-Vehicle (Bodhi's seed). In other words, the seed of the One Buddha-Vehicle has to be planted in the rich soil of Buddha-nature to reap the result of Buddhahood.

Hence, the Lotus Sutra is the Gift of the Law because the Buddha bestows the gift of the One Buddha-Vehicle to his disciples to continue the lineage of Supreme Perfect Enlightenment.

Figure 5: Gift of the Law toward Buddhahood

Conclusion

Wonderfully depicted through the Seven Parables, the One Buddha-Vehicle is the Gift of the Law by the Buddha. The One Buddha-Vehicle is also the Bodhi seed that has to be planted in the rich soil within our Buddha-nature (potentiality) in order for Buddhahood to be accomplished (outcome).

2 - Gift of Life (Buddha)
Overview: Understanding of the Gift of Life

There are two aspects to understanding the Gift of Life: first, revelation of the Dharmakaya of the Eternal Buddha expressed as the Four Virtues of True Self, Eternity, Purity, and Happiness[10] (wisdom); second, transmission of the Buddha's merits and achievements to support his disciples in attaining Buddhahood quickly (compassion). In other words, the wisdom aspect is the "what," and the compassion aspect is the "how."

The Buddha first declared his past attainment of Buddhahood eons ago as a way to covertly reveal his realization of the Dharmakaya of the Eternal Buddha through his personal experience. Then, the Buddha secretly shared the merits and virtues of his attainment to his disciples who responded joyously to his revelation, which denotes a secret process of life-to-life transmission of the Buddha's merits to support his disciples in attaining Buddhahood.

In short, the Gifts of Life are the bestowal of wisdom and compassion from the Buddha. By practicing the Lotus Sutra, disciples receive the merits and achievements of the Buddha to expedite the accomplishment of Supreme Perfect Enlightenment.

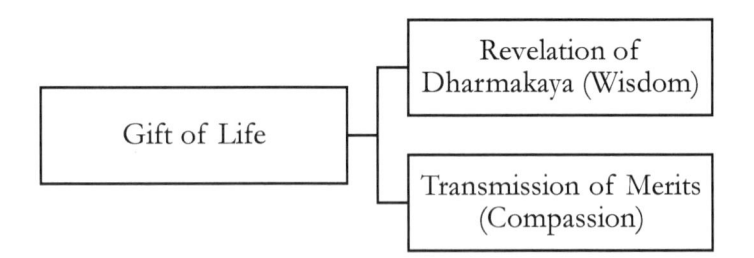

Table 7: Gift of Life in Terms of Wisdom and Compassion

Part 1 - Revelation of the Buddha's Dharmakaya (Wisdom)

A Buddha has three bodies (Trikaya): Dharmakaya (Truth/Dharma Body), Sambhogakaya (Reward/Transformation Body) and Nirmanakaya (Manifested/Physical Body).[11] Among the three bodies, Dharmakaya is the Buddha's ultimate true nature when he attains Supreme Perfect Enlightenment. In Digha Nikaya of the Pali Canon, Shakyamuni Buddha tells Vasettha that the Tathagata is the Dharmakaya, the "Truth-body," as well as Dharmabhuta, "Truth-become," that is, "One who has become the Truth."[12]

The Dharmakaya is also known as the Primordial Buddha, Adi Buddha, or Original Buddha. According to the Kagyu and Gelug lineages of Tibetan Buddhism, Vajradhara Buddha is the Primordial Buddha, or the Dharmakaya Buddha. In Tiantai and Hua-yen of the Chinese school, as well as Kegon, Shingon, and Tendai of the Japanese school, Vairocana Buddha is considered a Primordial Buddha. As for some of the Nichiren sects such as Nichiren Shoshu and Soka Gakkai, Nichiren himself is perceived as the Original Buddha.[13]

Zhiyi accorded primary importance to the Sambhogakaya (reward body) when he commented in Chapter 16, claiming that "the real intention is to discuss the merits of the reward body" based on his perception that "the reward body is to feel the throbbing life of the eternal Buddha in the midst of concrete, actual reality woven from joy and sadness, suffering and pleasure, good and evil."[14] I will explain in the following section why this is not quite right. The concept of the Eternal Buddha in Chapter 16 is actually the embodiment of Dharmakaya, not Sambhogakaya.

Dharmakaya Expressed as the Four Virtues

The Dharmakaya of a Buddha is expressed as the Four Virtues of True Self, Eternity, Purity, and Happiness, as taught in Mahayana Mahaparinirvana. We shall see later why the Lotus Sutra is an embodiment of the Dharmakaya of an Eternal and Universal Buddha through the personal experience of Shakyamuni Buddha.

45

In *The Sutra of Lion's Roar of Queen Srimala* (Śrīmālādevī Siṃhanāda Sūtra, 胜鬘狮子吼一乘大方便方广经), the Buddha illuminated the characteristics of the Buddha's Dharmakaya as having Four Virtues of True Self, Eternity, Purity, and Happiness:

> *The Dharmakaya of the Buddha has the perfection of permanence, the perfection of pleasure, the perfection of self, the perfection of purity. Whatever sentient beings see the Dharmakaya of the Tathagata that way, see correctly. Whoever see correctly are called the sons of the Lord born from his heart, born from his mouth, born from the Dharma, who behave as manifestations of Dharma and as heirs of Dharma.[14]*

Zhiyi interpreted the four Bodhisattvas of the Earth who appeared in the Lotus Sutra—Bodhisattva Superior Actions, Bodhisattva Boundless Actions, Bodhisattva Pure Actions, Bodhisattva Steadfast Actions—to denote the Four Virtues of True Self, Eternity, Purity, and Happiness respectively. While Zhiyi and Nichiren identified Chapter 2: Expedient Methods and Chapter 16: Eternal Lifespan of Tathagata as the core teachings of the Lotus Sutra, and the rest of the other chapters are considered as "branches and leaves of these two chapters,"[15] they did not explain that Chapter 16 encapsulates the Dharmakaya of Shakyamuni Buddha.

Chapter 16 is the essence of the Lotus Sutra because it embodies the life of Shakyamuni Buddha in the form of Dharmakaya of an Eternal Buddha. This means that Shakyamuni Buddha did not merely appear as the Nirmanakaya aspect of the Buddha through his human birth and attainment of enlightenment as "Shakyamuni Buddha," nor did he manifest himself as the Sambhogakaya aspect of the Buddha when he manifested resplendent bodily light and divine powers in Chapter 21: Divine Powers of Tathagata; he actually boldly declared his True Self as the Universal and Eternal Buddha who has everlasting lifespan, and he has never entered parinirvana.

To grasp the meaning of Dharmakaya through the Four Virtues of True Self, Eternity, Purity, and Happiness, we need to understand the meaning of the Four Virtues as expounded by the Buddha in Mahayana Mahaparinirvana Sutra:

> *"'The Self' signifies the Buddha; 'the Eternal' signifies the Dharmakaya; 'Bliss' signifies Nirvana; and 'the Pure' signifies Dharma."*[16]

Shakyamuni Buddha, through his revelation of his attainment of Buddhahood since the remote past and his eternal lifespan in Chapter 16, affirmed his achievement of the pure Dharma body. This is a testament that the Lotus Sutra is not just a teaching of Buddhahood but a veritable embodiment of the *wisdom* aspect of the Buddha in the form of the Dharmakaya of an Eternal Buddha who transcends the conventional concepts of name and form. In other words, the Buddha's Gift of Life is eternally preserved in the wisdom of his Dharma.

> *"It has been an immensely long period of time since I became a Buddha. My lifespan is immeasurable asamkhya kalpas. Eternal and immortal, I have always been dwelling here without ever entering parinirvana."*[17] *(LS 16: 1.13)*

Here is the understanding of the teaching of Eternal Buddha as the Dharmakaya of the Buddha in Mahayana Parinirvana Sutra:

> *"The body of the Tathagata is one that is eternal, one that is indestructible, and one that is adamantine, one that is not sustained by various kinds of food. It is the Dharma-Body."*[18]

Eternal Buddha is Not a Creator God of Monotheism

Some people may get the impression that the concept of Eternal Buddha is not different from the absolute, personal God of monotheism in Christianity as taught in the Bible and Hinduism as presented in the Bhagavad Gita. Although the Lotus Sutra recognizes the Brahma as the lord and Creator of the Threefold World (LS 1: 1.5, LS 23: 2.6), the Eternal Buddha is not at all regarded as the Creator but the *Uncreated*. The Buddha is a natural outcome arising from the transcendental transformation of the Dharma of Lotus that is beginningless and endless; it is not a type of "creation" in any material or physical sense.

Moreover, while Buddhist practitioners revere the Buddha, it is not a fanatical devotion (*bhakti*) to God unlike that in Hinduism or Abrahamic religions. The purpose of the Buddha's teaching is consistent: to devote oneself in the Dharma path of becoming a Buddha i.e. accomplishing Anuttara Samyak Sambodhi.

Implications

The implication of the Lotus Sutra being the embodiment of the Dharmakaya of an Eternal Buddha is that the imagery or depiction of "what a Buddha should look like"—be they Shakyamuni Buddha, Amitabha Buddha, Mahavairocana Buddha, or Vajradhara Buddha—are merely expedient means of expressing the truth of a Universal and Eternal Buddha who has achieved the Dharmakaya that transcends the concepts of name and form. Since all Buddhas in the Universe are the Dharmakaya of the Eternal Buddha, it is irrelevant which form of the Buddha you revere or embrace as part of your practice. This also means that, for those who do not fancy having a mandala or a Buddha's statue, they can use the book of the Lotus Sutra as an object of devotion itself because the sutra contains the life of the Buddha himself.

Conclusion

The wisdom aspect of the Gift of Life is the Dharmakaya of the Eternal Buddha, expressed as the Four Virtues of True Self, Eternity, Purity, and Happiness. Since the Lotus Sutra embodies the essence of the Buddha's life, practitioners of the Lotus Sutra are literally taking refuge in the Buddha just by embracing the sutra. The Buddha is not a Creator god but the Uncreated universal manifestation of the ultimate Dharma.

Part 2 - Transmission of Merits from the Buddha (Compassion)

The *compassion* aspect of the Gifts of Life are the merits, blessings, virtues, and fruits of attainments of the Buddha. After the Buddha revealed his attainment of Dharmakaya of the Eternal Buddha, he secretly and divinely transmitted his merits, virtues, and achievements to his disciples so as to support his disciples in quickly attaining Buddhahood. In other words, the Buddha's disciples literally *inherit* the immeasurable treasures directly from the Buddha himself. This very action is an expression of Buddha's profound generosity, grace, and compassion.

Secret Life-to-Life Transmission of Buddha's Merits

The process of transmission is mystical and transcendental as it involves the secret life-to-life "flowing" of Buddha's personal merits and fruits of achievement to his disciples through the medium of a sacred scripture. The Gift of the Law—the One Buddha-Vehicle—is already embedded within the depth of the Buddha's life. This Gift of the Law, together with the Gifts of Life in the form of merits and achievements, are shared by the Buddha with his disciples in a spiritually transcendental manner. As a consequence, the relationship and connection established between the Buddha and his disciples is eternal, transcending the boundaries of time and space.

Many Jataka tales document Shakyamuni Buddha's past practices of sacrificing his limbs and his lives for the sake of the Law. And yet, attaining Buddhahood is not assured. Let us face reality: attaining Buddhahood is by no means easy. One may be spending eons practicing morality and sacrifice, but there is no guarantee of realizing Supreme Perfect Enlightenment.

In one of the past lifetimes in which Shakyamuni Buddha was reborn as Bodhisattva Never Disrespectful, he learned about the Lotus Sutra from King of Majestic Voices Buddha. The Buddha declared and affirmed that "had I not accepted, embraced, read, recited, and expounded the Lotus Sutra for others, I would never have been able to attain Supreme Perfect Enlightenment so quickly" (LS 20: 1.15). Herein lies the critical teaching of the Lotus Sutra: it assures that one attains Buddhahood quickly.

The reality is that, without this spiritual transmission of merits from the Buddha to his disciples, it is virtually impossible for one to quickly attain Buddhahood through one's individual efforts in the shortest possible timeframe. While there should be no doubt that we all have the Buddha-nature within us (i.e., the potentiality for Buddhahood), if we receive no Bodhi seed in the form of One Buddha-Vehicle (Gift of the Law) and receive no divine support from the Buddha in the form of merits and prophecy of enlightenment (Gift of Life), then we are by no means assured of attaining Buddhahood. The giving of the Bodhi seed *and* transmission of the Buddha's merits are instrumental in supporting all his disciples to successfully achieve Supreme Perfect Enlightenment.

From the scriptural perspective, there is a continuation from Chapter 16 to Chapter 19. In fact, Chapter 17: Distinctions in Merits, Chapter 18: Merits of Spontaneous Joy in the Law, and Chapter 19: Merits of the Teachers of the Law, are all essentially transmissions of merits and benefits to the disciples as a result of hearing the teaching of the eternal lifespan, or Dharmakaya, from the Buddha. Let us review key scriptural evidence:

#1 – The Buddha Supports His Disciples to Attain Buddhahood

The Buddha's name is renowned in the ten directions for his generosity in bestowing benefits for all living beings. He develops their roots of benevolence so as to **support them in achieving unsurpassed wisdom.** *(LS 17: 1.25)*

#2 – Disciples Receive Great Benefits

At that time, when the great assembly heard the Buddha describing the length of his lifespan being such an extremely long period of time, immeasurably boundless asamkhya of living beings received great benefits. (LS 17: 1.1)

#3 – Disciples Receive Merits to Attain Buddhahood

O Ajita! Again, if there are people who understand the intricate meaning upon hearing the eternal lifespan of the Buddha, the merits they obtain will be infinite and they will be able to awaken to the unsurpassed wisdom of Tathagata. How much more so if they frequently hear the Lotus Sutra, teach others, embrace the sutra themselves or lead others to embrace, copy the sutra themselves or lead others to copy, and present flowers, incense, necklaces, streamers, banners, silk canopies, fragrant oil, or butter oil lamps as offerings to the scrolls of the sutras! With the immeasurably boundless merits gained, these people will be able to acquire the perfect wisdom. (LS 17: 3.1)

#4 – Purification of the Six Senses

At that time, the Buddha spoke to Bodhisattva-Mahasattva Ever Diligent: "If there are virtuous men and women who accept and embrace the Lotus Sutra by reading, reciting, explaining, expounding, copying, or transcribing it, these people will receive eight hundred merits for the eyes, twelve hundred merits for the ears, eight hundred merits for the nose, twelve hundred merits for the tongue, eight hundred merits for the body, and twelve hundred merits for the mind. These merits serve to adorn, cleanse, and purify their six senses. (LS 19: 1.1)

Importance of the Transmission of the Buddha's Lineage

In Tibetan Buddhism, the practice of guru devotion is a way to pass down the Buddha's lineage through a teacher. In contrast, the practice of the Lotus Sutra obviates the need for a teacher in a human form because the sutra itself is the ultimate teacher.

> *If there are living beings who, having accepted and believed in the Buddha-Bhagavat upon hearing the teaching of the Law, practice the Way diligently to seek the perfect wisdom, the Buddha-wisdom, the natural wisdom, **the teacherless wisdom**, the insight, power, and fearlessness of Tathagata... They are like the children who left the blazing house to receive the ox carriages. (LS 3: 4.25)*

It is not a well-known fact that transmission of the Buddha's lineage is pivotal in the Dharma practice. Shakyamuni Buddha has already transmitted his Buddha's lineage to Mahakashyapa who will then pass down Shakyamuni Buddha's lineage to Maitreya Buddha in the future. Even in the case of Maitreya Buddha, he needs to receive Shakyamuni Buddha's lineage through Mahakashyapa, who had received the Buddha's lineage from Shakyamuni Buddha. Here are the two important passages:

> *Then the Buddha said to all the bhiksus: "Do not say this. I now leave all the unsurpassed Dharma in the hands of Mahakasyapa. This Kasyapa will henceforth be the one upon whom you may rely. This is as in the case where the Tathagata becomes the one to whom all beings can turn. The same is the case with Mahakasyapa. He will now become your refuge. This is as in the case of a king who has many territories and who goes on a tour of inspection, leaving all affairs of state in the hands of his minister. The same with the Tathagata. All right*

teachings are left in the hands of Mahakasyapa."– Mahayana Mahaparinirvana Sutra.[19]

In Maitreya Buddha, after his attainment of Buddhahood, will find Mahakashyapa seated in deep samadhi meditation in the Wolf Track Mountain.[20] Mahakashayapa will then pass the Dharma robe worn by Shakyamuni Buddha and offer it to Maitreya Buddha, saying: "The great teacher Shakyamuni, the Tathagata, Arhat, Samyak-Sambuddha, upon His parinirvana, entrusted me with His Dharma robe and commanded me to offer it to the World-Honored One." - Sutra of Bodhisattva Maitreya's Attainment of Buddhahood as Pronounced by the Buddha.[21]

As you can see, this action of passing down the Dharma robe of Shakyamuni Buddha is a symbolic transmission of the Buddha's lineage from one Buddha to the next to ensure continuation and legitimacy of the Dharma inheritance.

The practice of Dharma hinges upon the connection between a Buddha and his disciple, or a Dharma teacher and his disciple. The relationship between a Buddha and his disciple or a Dharma master and disciple is eternal, as the disciples will always be reborn with the same Buddha or Dharma teacher to practice the Dharma in the future lifetimes. Here is the scriptural evidence:

The Buddha said to the monks: "These sixteen bodhisattvas have always joyously expounded the Lotus Sutra, teaching and transforming six hundred trillion nayuta of Ganges's sands of living beings. Lifetime after lifetime, living beings are reborn in company with those bodhisattvas. Upon hearing the Law, they are able to have faith and understanding in the Law. As a result of these causes and conditions, they are able to encounter four hundred trillion Buddhas-Bhagavats, never ceasing until the present moment. (LS 7: 4.12)

After that Buddha had entered parinirvana,
those who heard the Law
would dwell in the various Buddha-lands,
always reborn together with their teachers. (LS 7: 6.23)

If there are disciples
who stay close to Teachers of the Law,
who follow and learn from their teachers,
they will meet Buddhas as numerous as the Ganges's sands.
to quickly attain the bodhisattva way. (LS 10: 2.28)

Formal Entrustment of Dharma

The transmission of merits from the Buddha to his disciples is not limited to secret transmission per se because, in Chapter 22: Entrustment, we see the formal "public" entrustment of the Dharma to exhort his disciples and spread the Lotus Sutra widely. This entrustment completes the transference of the Dharma Seal of the Buddha's lineage.

Scriptural-Based Practice to Attain Buddhahood

In the absence of the sutra and when people are mostly illiterate, practitioners actually receive the Buddha's lineage through reverence and devotion to Buddhist monks, masters, or teachers. However, if the sutras are widely available and most people are well-educated to read and write, having Dharma teachers in a physical *human* form is no longer necessary because the sutra that contains the life of the Buddha is the Teacher.

As such, the implication of the compassionate transmission of the Buddha's merits via the Lotus Sutra is that a Dharma teacher in a physical human form is no longer necessary because one can directly connect with the Buddha's Eternal Life, virtues, and merits through practicing the scripture itself. By performing activities such as accepting, reading, reciting the Lotus Sutra, chanting the title of the Lotus Sutra, and explaining and sharing the teachings of the Lotus Sutra with others, your mind with be one with the Buddha's mind. That is why the Buddha repeatedly urges his disciples to single-mindedly practice the way of Buddhahood by means of the Lotus Sutra.

This is a testament of the "Special Method" of the Lotus Sutra, because the practice toward Buddhahood has shifted from the practice of morality (that adheres by the Law of Causality) as taught in the Pali Canon to the practice of devotion (that adheres to the Law of Emptiness) as taught in the Lotus Sutra. This also means that the Law of Emptiness through the grace of the Buddha supersedes the inexorable Law of Cause and Effect.

Conclusion

The compassion aspect, the Gifts of Life, are the Buddha's merits and virtues which are secretly transmitted by the Buddha to support his disciples in attaining Buddhahood quickly.

The Lotus Sutra encapsulates the merits of the Dharmakaya of an Eternal Buddha through the personal experience of Shakyamuni Buddha. By practicing the Lotus Sutra, all Buddha's disciples will receive the merits and achievements of the Buddha to expedite their accomplishment of Supreme Perfect Enlightenment.

By virtue of the divine powers inherent in the Lotus Sutra itself, a physical teacher in a human form is not necessary. Disciples can attain Buddhahood through the scriptural-based practice of the Lotus Sutra owing to the establishment of relationship between a Buddha and his disciple while single-mindedly focusing on practicing this one special scripture.

3 - *Gift of Love (Sangha)*

In the context of the Three Gifts, all the gifts are externally bestowed by the Buddhas and bodhisattvas. Therefore, the Gift of Love means the gift of divine salvation by Bodhisattva Avalokitesvara. However, from the application perspective, the compassionate actions of Buddhas and bodhisattvas can be our models to cultivate the gift of compassion within our hearts.

Divine Salvation by Bodhisattva Avalokitesvara

The title of Chapter 25 of the Lotus Sutra is "Universal Gateway of Bodhisattva Avalokitesvara." This title denotes that the practice of Bodhisattva Avalokitesvara is a universal point of access to the Dharma. In Tibetan Buddhism, Bodhisattva Avalokitesvara, also known as Chenrezig, is an important meditational deity. The Dalai Lama is said to be the embodiment of Bodhisattva Avalokitesvara.

Bodhisattva Avalokitesvara is the personification of profound compassion, divine grace, and unconditional love. He protects and saves immeasurable people who are tormented by suffering in the midst of adversity and calamity.

The Buddha taught his disciples to single-mindedly call upon and pay homage to this bodhisattva. By having faith in the divine powers and profound compassion of Bodhisattva Avalokitesvara for salvation, we can connect our hearts and minds to this bodhisattva for support and assistance. The practice of relying upon Bodhisattva Avalokitesvara for salvation is a method of tapping upon Tariki, or Other-Power, of an enlightened spiritual being. By having a balance between self-efforts to achieve enlightenment and the support from "Other-Power" in times of need, we are more empowered to develop our inner compassion to enable others to attain enlightenment as well.

The Essence of Love in Four Immeasurables

The Four Immeasurables, also known as Brahmaviharas which means "the abodes of the Brahma," are the Buddha's teachings on cultivating the "Heart-ware" of a human being. The Four Immeasurables are benevolence (loving-kindness), compassion, joy, and equanimity (non-attachment). Differences of the four qualities are shown in the table below:

Four Immeasurables	Differentiation of Virtuous Qualities	Types of Negative Tendencies to Eliminate
Benevolence (kindness)	Giving something of value to others (generosity)	Ego, selfishness, greed
Compassion	Removing or alleviating suffering in people (purification)	Cruelty, hatred, anger
Joy	Sharing the joy and celebrating success experienced by others (generosity)	Resentment, envy, jealousy
Equanimity (non-attachment)	Relinquishing and letting go of unwholesome habits and experiences (purification)	Apathy, prejudice, craving, obsession

Table 8: Love as the Four Immeasurables

Chapters 23 to 28, in addition to Chapter 20 of the Lotus Sutra, provide concrete examples of how a bodhisattva practice of the Dharma of loving-kindness and compassion leads toward achieving enlightenment. The following table is the overview of the qualities and virtues displayed by different bodhisattvas who appear in selective chapters of the Lotus Sutra:

Chapters	Virtues/Qualities
Chapter 20: Bodhisattva Never Disrespectful	Patience, Endurance, Perseverance
Chapter 23: History of Bodhisattva Medicine King	Devotion, Sacrifice, Generosity
Chapter 24: Bodhisattva Wonderful Music	Generosity, Joy
Chapter 25: Universal Gateway of Bodhisattva Avalokitesvara	Grace, Compassion, Generosity
Chapter 26: Dharani	Protection, Support, Generosity
Chapter 27: History of King Magnificent Glory	Compassion, Filial Piety, Joy
Chapter 28: Encouragement of Bodhisattva Universal Worthy	Protection, Support, Generosity

Table 9: Virtues of the Bodhisattvas in Practicing the Dharma

Bodhisattva Never Disrespectful (Chapter 20)

Bodhisattva Never Disrespectful was a past life of Shakyamuni Buddha. The practices of this bodhisattva were geared toward asceticism, discipline, gentleness, patience, sacrifice, and endurance. For innumerable past lifetimes, Shakyamuni Buddha had been practicing predominantly ascetic and personal sacrificial practices for the sake of Dharma. [22]

Bodhisattva Medicine King (Chapter 23)

Bodhisattva Medicine King practiced unflinching devotion to the Dharma by constantly giving offerings to the Buddha. His spirit of generosity went to the extent of sacrificing his limb and life for the sake of the Buddha.

However, Shakyamuni Buddha taught that the merits of offering one's body cannot compare with the immeasurable merits of embracing one verse of the Lotus Sutra. [23] The practice of the Lotus Sutra has the most supreme merits because embracing the Lotus Sutra is tantamount to giving offerings to all Buddhas.

Bodhisattva Wonderful Music (Chapter 24)

Talented and passionate about music, Bodhisattva Wonderful Music practiced generosity through offering music to the Buddha. By being authentic to one's strengths and interests, this bodhisattva practiced the Dharma with joy.

Moreover, he enjoyed forging friendship and acquaintance with bodhisattvas from other lands by attending the assembly of the Lotus Sutra expounded by Shakyamuni Buddha. He brought his followers along to the assembly, benefiting all of them. From here we learn that forging friendship and bringing a friend to a Dharma talk are all expressions of generosity and kindness.

Dharani (Chapter 26)

Another way to practice compassion is by supporting our Dharma friends and communities. The Dharani chapter tells how different types of beings offer spiritual protection in the form of a divine mantra to protect the practitioners of the Lotus Sutra. Thus, protecting and supporting the Sangha through monetary donation and volunteerism are all expressions of generosity and compassion.

History of King Magnificent Glory (Chapter 27)

As the saying goes, blood is thicker than water. The importance of family and kinship cannot be overemphasized in the journey of attaining Buddhahood.

King Magnificent Glory was a follower of the Brahman's teachings while his two sons, Pure Treasure and Pure Sight, were the Buddha's disciples. To convince his father to embrace the Buddha's teachings, the two sons performed supernatural acts which were manifestations of their spiritual achievements. Impressed and delighted upon seeing the supernatural feats, King Magnificent Glory was convinced of the power of Buddha's teachings. He subsequently practiced the Buddha-Dharma and attained Buddhahood.

King Magnificent Glory attained Buddhahood through the unconditional love and filial piety displayed by his two sons, who never gave up in guiding their father to practice the Buddha's teachings. This is a testament that relationship, kinship, and friendships are critical factors leading us to achieve enlightenment.

Encouragement of Bodhisattva Universal Worthy (Chapter 28)

Bodhisattva Universal Worthy provided encouragement and support to the Buddha's disciples by offering protection to the practitioners of the Lotus Sutra. He also supported Shakyamuni Buddha in the propagation of the Lotus Sutra by ensuring widespread propagation of the Lotus Sutra through his vows and divine powers. The support, protection, and encouragement offered by this bodhisattva are manifestations of generosity and compassion.

Cultivate Compassion within Our Hearts

When it comes to the actual practice, compassion becomes the bedrock of Buddhism. The virtue of compassion has multi-faceted qualities: love, kindness, grace, patience, benevolence, endurance, forgiveness, acceptance, generosity, etc. Each one represents a different aspect of compassion.

The linchpin of a bodhisattva practice is none other than compassionate actions. By lending a helping hand to those around us, we can cultivate the spirit of Bodhisattva Avalokitesvara in our daily lives. Doing charity work and volunteering for non-profit organizations that help the underprivileged are some of the ways we can spread kindness and compassion in our community.

If we look deeper, we will understand that the essence of love and compassion arises from our relationship with people. People we meet in our lives—be they parents, spouse, children, bosses, subordinates, friends, classmates, or spiritual teachers—greatly influence whether or not we eventually encounter the Dharma. This underscores the significant role of relationships, friendships, and kinships for attaining Buddhahood. We can develop compassion by becoming mindful of the ways in which we can be of service to others in our daily lives.

Conclusion

The Gift of Love has two aspects: first, the gift of divine salvation by Bodhisattva Avalokitesvara; second, the gift of compassion cultivated within our hearts. By having faith and devotion to Bodhisattva Avalokitesvara, we receive protection and deliverance from suffering in times of calamity. By cultivating the qualities of compassion within our hearts, we spread loving-kindness and compassion to the people around us.

Section 2:

Buddha in the Sky

Doctrines of Past Buddhist Masters

The Doctrines of Nagarjuna

Nagarjuna, founder of Madhyamaka Buddhism, relied upon the Prajnaparamita Sutras as his primary texts to explain the meaning of Emptiness, Dependent Origination, and the Middle Way.

According to Nagarjuna, emptiness means "things exist but their existence is never self-standing. The existence of entities is always dependent on many conditions."[1] For example, a sunflower must have such causes and conditions as the sunflower seed, sun, water, air, and earth in order for it to grow. An airplane is a combination of the steel, plastic, engines, rubber, and thousands of other components that enable it to exist. Without these individual parts, there is no airplane, which means it is empty of independent existence. These examples reflect the interconnectedness of all phenomena, and they are the expressions of the principle of Dependent Origination.

Nagarjuna declared that Emptiness and Dependent Origination are synonymous.[2] He further explained the Middle Way (Madhyamaka) to be the recognition that "all things exist dependently; they are not the extremes of nihilism (all things are non-existent in reality) and eternalism (things in reality have existence independent of conditions)."[3]

Zhiyi's Threefold Truths

In Tiantai Buddhism, the doctrine of the Threefold Truths is considered the magnum opus of Zhiyi because most of his subsequent theories revolve around the Threefold Truths. For instance, doctrines such as Three Delusions, Threefold Contemplation in One Mind, and meditation practices as outlined in *Great Concentration and Insight* have their foundation upon the Threefold Truths.[4] Let us review the philosophy of Threefold Truths:

#1 – The Truth of Emptiness (ku 空谛)

In Sanskrit, Emptiness or Voidness is known as Shunyata. All phenomena are said to be empty because they are impermanent and do not have an independent reality of their own. This means that all Dharma cannot exist on its own because phenomena are causally produced by other conditions. In other words, they co-arise dependently.

#2 – The Truth of Falseness (ke 假谛)

In Sanskrit, Falseness is known as Samvrtisatya, or "empirical truth." Although all Dharma are empty, they do have a temporary or provisional existence as perceived by the six senses. This means that phenomena are perceived to have a "concrete" but impermanent existence.

#3 – The Truth of the Middle Way (chu 中谛)

In Sanskrit, the Middle Way is known as Madhyama. This means that Truth #1 and Truth #2 are both empty and also have temporary existence at the same time. The Middle Way should not be understood as lying between the two, but as identical with them; they are inseparable and essentially the same.

Zhiyi used the Confucian terminology of 'Li' and 'Shih' to explain the Middle Way. While the phenomena ('Shih') remain distinct, they are identical in terms of emptiness, and therefore all phenomena are parts of the one single unity of Law ('Li'). This means that they are all perfectly integrated: one-in-three and three-in-one.

Buddha in the Sky = Three Ultimate Truths

The theoretical Buddhist doctrines explained by or derived from Buddhist masters are often contradictory, complex, and confusing. Truth be told, I myself am not spared from this "philosophical conundrum."

Zhiyi derived his understanding of the Emptiness, Dependent Origination, and Middle Way from Nagarjuna. Contemplating Zhiyi's Threefold Truths, my mind kept asking, "Since Truth #1 and Truth #2 are essentially identical, and Truth #3 is to affirm that all three of them are 'empty and temporary,' then how do we explain the Dharmakaya of Buddhahood—an eternal state of birthlessness and deathlessness—that is not dependently co-arisen?" The way in which Nagarjuna and Zhiyi explain the doctrines leave plenty of questions about the true nature of Buddhahood, because they did not explain how these doctrines are connected to the Mahayana teaching of intrinsic nature (Skt. Svabhava) or Buddha-nature (Skt. Tathagatagarbha). In fact, Nagarjuna's refutation of "eternalism" runs counter with the nature of Eternity of Buddhahood.

When I looked deep into my heart and listened to my inner voice to seek intuitive understanding of the theory, I felt something was not "aligned." This spiritual dissonance propelled me to seek the truth of the Buddha-Dharma.

On the evening of 10 July 2017, while I was chanting the daimoku in front of the Gohonzon, three Chinese characters—"Kong Zhong Fo" (空中佛), which means "Buddha in the Sky"—just popped to my mind like a bolt out of the blue. I quickly wrote down the "divine revelation" in my notepad.

As I reviewed my three characters later, the image of "Buddha in the Sky" reminded me of the image of "Ceremony in the Air" in which Seven-Jeweled Treasure Pagoda of the Abundant Treasure Buddha suddenly emerged from the earth and was suspended in mid-air (Chapter 11 to 22). Moreover, I also remembered that Bodhisattva Never Disrespectful received the teaching of the Lotus Sutra from the King of Majestic Voices *in the sky* (Chapter 20).

It dawned on me that, if each of the three characters are understood separately, "Kong" (空) means Emptiness, "Zhong" (中) means the Middle Way, and "Fo" (佛) means Buddhahood. It didn't take me long to realize that these three characters are deceptively similar but significantly different from Zhiyi's Threefold Truths of Emptiness, Falseness and the Middle Way. You might have spotted the difference now: the only critical difference between Zhiyi's Threefold Truth and my "Buddha in the Sky" is the *Truth of Buddhahood*.

Three Truths	Zhiyi's Threefold Truths	Buddha in the Sky
Truth 1	Emptiness 空 (Kong)	Emptiness 空 (Kong)
Truth 2	Middle Way 中 (Zhong)	Middle Way 中 (Zhong)
Truth 3	Falseness 假 (Jia)	Buddhahood 佛 (Fo)

Figure 6: Differences between Tian Tai's Threefold Truths and My Three Ultimate Truths

Truth #1: The Law of Emptiness

The doctrine of Emptiness is found in many Mahayana sutras such as *the Perfection of Wisdom Sutra, the Heart Sutra, the Diamond Sutra, Shurangama Samadhi Sutra, the Vimalakirti Sutra,* and so on. Also known as voidness or non-substantiality, the doctrine of Emptiness is one of the most intellectually perplexing Buddhist philosophies. In Tibetan Buddhism, Emptiness is one of the three core teachings, the other two being bodhicitta (aspiration for Buddhahood) and renunciation.[5]

The Law of Emptiness is expounded in the Lotus Sutra as well. You may refer to *Appendix 2: Quotes of Emptiness in the Threefold Lotus Sutra* to find out more about the quotes related to Emptiness. The closing sutra of the Lotus Sutra, *The Sutra of Meditation on Bodhisattva Universal Worthy*, is a teaching about the meditation on emptiness as a method of repentance for the purification of unwholesome karma.

Nagarjuna perceived Emptiness as synonymous with Dependent Origination and the Middle Way. However, I will show you why the Law of Emptiness is not Dependent Origination or the Middle Way. To be specific, Emptiness is Eternity, not impermanence. The Law of Emptiness is the truth of the unconditional world beyond the realm of creation and birth. In other words, the Law of Emptiness is equivalent to the Law of Buddhahood. We can revolutionize our understanding of Emptiness in a concrete way through three alternative perspectives:

- Emptiness is Infinity
- Emptiness is Purity
- Emptiness is Eternity

1. Emptiness is Infinity

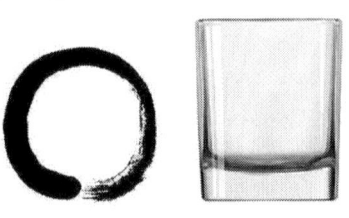

Figure 7: Enso Circle and the Receptacle

In Zen/Chan Buddhism, an *enso* circle is used to represent Emptiness. The round *enso* circle is like a round glass cup, an empty receptacle or a container that is capable of holding objects within itself. With these two objects as metaphors, we can imagine Emptiness as the "vessel" of an infinite empty space. This does not mean that Emptiness is "nothingness." Emptiness is an entity in itself.

An empty space has no inherent physical characteristic; it is formless and non-dual, unlike physical objects that have different shapes, colours, and sizes. Just like the empty space inside a receptacle, the Law of Emptiness can be imagined to be a vast empty space, environment, field, or realm. Thus, it can also be understood as a state of potentiality such as the Buddha-nature, which is the potentiality to become a Buddha, and Dharmadhatu, which means the realm of the Dharma. In short, Emptiness is the truth of Infinity.

The Buddha in the state of Dharmakaya is formless and non-dual. The imagery depictions of the Buddhas and bodhisattvas in the form of statues and paintings are merely expedient representations of the Buddhas and bodhisattvas. In fact, the same Buddha can appear in different places as a different person with a different form and name for the purpose of leading one to enlightenment. Hence, the state and transformation of the Buddha's life is infinite, just like a vast empty space.

Here are some of the quotes related to empty space and Emptiness as the truth of infinity in the Threefold Lotus Sutra:

*If any bodhisattvas wish to practice and learn the Immeasurable Meanings, then they should observe and perceive that all realities are originally—from the beginning and continue to be—empty and tranquil in nature and aspect. There is neither large nor small, neither birth nor death, neither abiding nor moving, neither advancing nor retreating, just **like an empty space with no dualism.** (Immeasurable Meanings Sutra 2: 1.6)*

I have also seen some bodhisattvas
who view the nature of all phenomena
as having non-dual characteristics
just like an empty space.
(LS 1: 2.45)

They should perceive the Law
as having no substantiality,
like an empty space,
without a firm solidity—
no birth, no emerging,
no movement, no regression.
Perceiving the eternal unity of one single form
is what I called the appropriate associations.
(LS 14: 2.17)

2. Emptiness Is Purity

Emptiness carries the meaning of purity. The Law of Emptiness works like a "spiritual vacuum cleaner" with great suction power to cleanse and purify all karmic impediments, dirt and grime. Karmic obscuration is a cause of suffering. By eliminating the negative karma and impure thought, speech, and actions, happiness will follow "like a shadow that never leave him."[6] Thus, quality of purity and happiness are inseparable.

In *the Sutra of Meditation on Bodhisattva Universal Worthy*, the Buddha taught his disciples the visualization method anchored upon the Law of Emptiness to expiate unwholesome karma accumulated in incalculable past lifetimes. You may refer to *Appendix 4: Ten Quotes of Emptiness from The Sutra of Meditation on Bodhisattva Universal Worthy* for more quotes about purification of unwholesome karma through meditating upon the Law of Emptiness. In sum, the Law of Emptiness is a method of spiritual healing for the purpose of attaining Buddhahood. Here are some highlighted quotes:

> "...*By practicing repentance in this way, you will achieve purification of your body and mind.*" *(MBUW 7.5)*

> "...*recite the Great Vehicle sutra, and ponder upon the profound Law of Emptiness of the foremost in meaning and principle, then it only takes the time of a snap of a finger for them to eliminate the sins of birth and death accumulated over hundreds of millions of billions of asamkhya kalpas.*" *(MBUW 9.4)*

> "...*they should diligently read and practice this equal and impartial sutra, ponder the profound Law of Emptiness—the foremost in meaning—in order to connect their minds with the wisdom of emptiness. You should know that these people will completely eliminate all their sins and transgressions forever through every instant of their meditative thoughts.*" *(MBUW 9.11)*

> *The Buddha spoke to Ananda: "I, along with the bodhisattvas in the Wise Kalpa and the Buddhas in the ten directions, am able to wipe out the sins of birth and death accumulated over hundreds of millions of billions of asamkhya kalpas as a result of pondering the true meaning of the Great Vehicle." (MBUW 9.2)*

3. Emptiness is Eternity

Apart from purification, the Law of Emptiness also has the hidden meaning of Eternity, a characteristic of Buddhahood. In Chapter 16, the Buddha declared his eternal lifespan as a Dharmakaya Buddha. The everlasting life of a Buddha is the True Self of a Buddha.

The Chinese characters "Wu Liang Wu Bian" （无量无边） means immeasurable, boundless, and infinite. The state of infinity means Eternity—the state of birthlessness and deathlessness that has no beginning or end. This is the realm of the Extinction in Great Nirvana. The Dharmakaya state of Buddhahood is not dependently co-arisen, therefore, as opposed to the nature of impermanence that exists in a conditioned world, the nature of Buddhahood is an eternal and permanent realm of an unconditional and uncreated realm:

> *"Why is this so? Because Tathagata completely perceives the true characteristics of the Threefold World as they are: there is no birth or death, no ebbing or arising. Neither is there present existence and subsequent extinction, substantial reality or fictitious imagination, same or different. These characteristics of realities are not what one perceives them to be while living in the Threefold World. Tathagata has clearly and unmistakably seen all these." (LS 16: 1.11)*

We are living in a conditioned world in which the impermanence lies in the physical realm of materialism. Everything is in constant flux; phenomena that arise in one moment will vanish the next. Thus, the Abrahamic doctrine of divine creation by a Supreme Being is intrinsically fallacious and misguided. We need to perceive the truth of impermanence in the ever-changing world of forms in order to understand the truth of eternity in the Uncreated world of transformation in the lotus.

Eternity is the state of birthlessness and deathlessness. The marvel of the Buddha's teaching is the focus, not the Creator or the created, but the Uncreated. We should not focus on the Creator, but upon the Uncreated, and hence the undestroyed and the undestroyable. Where there is no beginning, there is no ending. Where there is no creation, there is no destruction. This is the true meaning of eternity, the true meaning of Buddhahood.

Application of the Law of Emptiness in Life

Apart from the role it plays in purifying past negative karma, the Law of Emptiness is also a creative Law that knows no limits or boundaries. Emptiness means infinity, purity, and eternity. This means that our potential within us is infinite and, therefore, we should not limit ourselves to preconceived notions of what we can achieve as an individual.

Emptiness also teaches us to go back to the basics by living simply. The Zen of simplicity is the source of abundant joy. By reducing our consumption and materialistic cravings, we can learn to savour the joys and the beauty that money cannot buy: nature, deeper connection with people, gratitude for what we have, and the bliss that comes from meditation, just to name a few. Minimalism is the new black.

In the area of business, the Law of Emptiness can also be applied. Emptiness is like a receptacle or empty space that contains all there is. For example, businesses such as Facebook, Uber, AirBnB, and Amazon are all platforms that do not "own" any people, vehicles, rooms or products; they merely provide seemingly infinite "space" for people to gather together for a specific services or products.

Emptiness, being non-dual and having no inherent nature of its own, also means non-judgment. While it is essential and beneficial to differentiate between good and bad and right and wrong, it is important to recognize that things change when external conditions change. What is considered to be good or right can suddenly become wrong and evil. Thus, sometimes, it is worthwhile to practice acceptance and let go of judgment, especially self-judgment that does not lead to the development of healthy self-esteem.

Besides, Emptiness means being mindful at the present moment rather than dwelling in the past and future. In Emptiness, there is no duality of past and present—only the eternal present moment. By meditating upon Emptiness, we are abiding upon the awareness of the present moment in its fullest. Hence, practicing the meditation of Emptiness is no different from mindfulness meditation as taught in the Satipatthana Sutta.

Conclusion

Emptiness can be understood in three different ways: first, Emptiness as Infinity; second, Emptiness as Purity, and third, Emptiness as Eternity.

Like a vast empty space or environment with no inherent physical characteristics, Emptiness is non-dual, formless, and infinite. Emptiness can thus be understood as the potentiality of Buddhahood (Buddha-nature) and the realm of the Dharma (Dharmadhatu).

Emptiness is purity. It is a method to purify one's karmic imprints for the purpose of spiritual healing toward Buddhahood. Purity is the prerequisite of happiness.

Emptiness is eternity. The Eternal Buddha in the state of Dharmakaya has an everlasting lifespan and that is the True Self of a Buddha. Thus, Supreme Perfect Enlightenment is an uncreated state of birthlessness and deathlessness in an unconditioned world.

Truth #2: The Law of the Middle Way

Both Nagarjuna and Zhiyi interpreted the theory of the Middle Way in relation to the doctrine of Emptiness: all phenomena are empty of any inherent independent nature because they are all dependently co-arisen, resulting in their impermanent existence. Nagarjuna explained the Middle Way as "all things exist dependently; they are not the extremes of nihilism and eternalism."

Nevertheless, Zhiyi expanded the Ten Factors or Ten Suchness, a principle of Dependent Origination, to derive his new theory of Ichinen Sanzen, which was subsequently adopted hook, line and sinker by Nichiren. In fact, Nichiren regarded Ichinen Sanzen as the "fundamental principle of the Lotus Sutra"[7] and "the very essence of the Buddha's teachings."[8]

Ichinen Sanzen

Ichinen Sanzen （一念三千）or "Three Thousand Realms in a Single Moment of Life" is a celebrated doctrine created by Zhiyi. This doctrine explains that life at any moment has infinite possibilities because the state of Buddhahood is not separable from ordinary being.

I always struggle to find philosophical resonance with the doctrine of Ichinen Sanzen. This is because, innovative though the doctrine is, it distracts us from perceiving the One Buddha-Vehicle as the essence of the Lotus Sutra. Let me explain the reasons why Ichinen Sanzen is not entirely the "very essence of the Buddha's teachings" as claimed by Nichiren.

Ichinen Sanzen is a "derived" doctrine composed of three factors: Ten Worlds, Ten Factors, and Three Realms.

Ichinen Sanzen (3,000 Realms in a Single Moment of Life) = 10 Worlds x 10 Worlds x 10 Factors x 3 Realms of Existence[9]

Ten Factors

The description of the Ten Factors or Ten Suchness is found in Chapter 2 of the Lotus Sutra.[10] Broadly speaking, the Ten Factors are essentially the Law of Cause and Effect and are intricately connected with the doctrine of Dependent Origination or Twelve-linked Chains of Causation. The Ten Factors are Appearance, Nature, Entity, Power, Influence, Internal Cause, Relation, Latent Effect, Manifest Effect, and the Consistency from Beginning to the End.

While the Ten Factors can be traced back to the Lotus Sutra, this doctrine is not the crux of the Buddha's teachings. Why?

Chapter 2 can be segmented into two parts: the "provisional" part before the 5,000 disciples left the assembly, and the "essential" part after the 5,000 disciples left the assembly. Since the Ten Factors was expounded by the Buddha before the 5,000 disciples left the assembly, it means that Ten Factors is actually a "provisional" teaching. The core teaching is the One Buddha-Vehicle that was expounded by the Buddha after the 5,000 disciples had left the assembly.[11] Thus, including the "provisional" teaching of Ten Factors renders Ichinen Sanzen to be "provisional" in nature.

Moreover, the Sanskrit versions of the Lotus Sutra list only five elements, instead of Ten Factors:[12]

> *Only the Thus Come One knows all the dharmas: what are the dharmas, how are the dharmas, what are the dharmas like, of what characteristics are the dharmas, of what nature are the dharmas; what they are, how they are, what they are like, of what characteristics they are, of what nature are the dharmas, only the Thus Come One has had direct experience in those dharmas.[13]*

As such, focusing on the Ten Factors (which in the Sanskrit and Chinese translations differ in the number of "factors") further diminishes the value and validity of the doctrine.

Ten Worlds

The Ten Worlds cannot be traced back in the Lotus Sutra, but they are implicit in the Mahayana doctrines, and they can be found in the commentaries written by Buddhist masters (secondary sources.) The Ten Worlds are: Hell, Hungry Spirits (Hunger), Beasts (Animality), Asura (Anger), Humans (Humanity), Heaven (Rapture), Shravaka (Learning), Pratyekabuddha (Realization), Bodhisattva, and Buddhahood.[14]

The Ten Worlds are repeated twice in the equation to explain the concept of the "Mutual Possessions of the Ten Worlds" (十界互具). The essence of this theory is that life has infinite possibilities and potential at any present moment, which means that we can experience any of the Ten Worlds in our lives. In other words, at any given moment, the Buddha's realm contains the other nine states, therefore the state of Buddhahood is not separated from the ordinary beings.

Three Realms

The Three Realms are: (1) the realm of the five components, (2) the realm of living beings and (3) the realm of the environment. The source of the Three Realms is not found in the Lotus Sutra. Instead, it appears in the secondary source written by Nagarjuna, *The Treatise on the Great Perfection of Wisdom* (Skt: Mahaprajnaparamita-shastra, Chn: 大智度论).[15]

The name "three thousand" in Ichinen Sanzen reminds us of another term—Three Thousand Major Thousandfold World (三千大千世界)—that appears frequently in the Lotus Sutra. I often wonder: why would I use a definite number such as "three thousand" (三千) to explain the concept of infinity when I can use the word "immeasurable" (无量无边) instead? Moreover, Zhiyi's interpretation of the power "a single experience,"[16] based on his theory of Ichinen Sanzen, makes one wonder if it is necessary to derive a complex theory just to explain the power of being mindful of the present moment?

In short, Zhiyi's Ichinen Sanzen is a theory derived from Ten Factors, a doctrine of Dependent Origination or the Law of Causality, to explain the potentiality and mutual possession of all life forms in the Ten Worlds. The problem with this theory is that it focuses on the Ten Factors, which are provisional in nature, as the primary components of the equation. The prominence of this theory has somewhat eclipsed us from perceiving the truth of the One Buddha-Vehicle, which was revealed later in Chapter 2 when 5,000 disciples had left the congregation.

How I Understand the Law of the Middle Way

From the perspective of Dharma, Nagarjuna perceived the Middle Way in terms of Emptiness and Dependent Origination, and Zhiyi interpreted the Middle Way as the "unification of Emptiness and Falseness." On the contrary, I prefer to understand the meaning of the Middle Way as the manifestations of the *conditioned* world in two ways:

1) The Middle Way is the Truth of Skillful Means
2) The Middle Way is the Truth of Law of Cause and Effects

1. The Middle Way is the Truth of Skillful Means

Figure 8: Marbles in the Container to Illustrate the Middle Way

The Middle Way can be understood to be an object—with its different shapes, colours, and sizes—inside a receptacle. All life forms in the Ten Worlds are manifestations of the Law of the Middle Way. Every unique life form with its distinctive characteristic is itself the Middle Way. For example, all living beings such as the plants, animals, and human livings with their immeasurable shapes, colours, and sizes are the Middle Way. Essentially, all living beings in the threefold realms of Desire, Form, and Formlessness belong to the Middle Way.

The same applies to the Buddha's teachings. The Buddha understood the importance of contextualized teaching according to the needs of individuals and the suitability in different circumstances. This method of teaching is called "skillful means" or "expedient methods." As such, all the Buddha's teachings are the Dharma of the Middle Way.

Shakyamuni Buddha realized the importance of the Middle Way in the voyage of enlightenment. After the Buddha left his palaces in pursuit of a spiritual life, he chose the path of an extreme, ascetic life by eating only one hemp seed per day. Not soon after, he lost his golden glow; his face became haggard, and his body was terribly emaciated. Eventually, Buddha was awakened to the truth that, in a conditioned world, the practice of extremism is unwise and impractical. As a human being (an object of the Middle Way in itself), the practice of the Middle Way is the path to realize Buddhahood.

The teachings of the Middle Way abound in the Pali Canon. Once, the Buddha taught his disciple Sona the wisdom of the Middle Way through the metaphor of a zither. Sona was a cheerful and diligent disciple who faced a bottleneck in his Dharma practice because he exerted himself beyond his personal limits. The Buddha used the tautness of the zither's string—not too tight and not too loose—to explain the concept of the Middle Way to guide Sona in his practice.

The Noble Eightfold Path is regarded as the Middle Path (Majjhima-patipada) because it is a practice that avoids the two extremes of sensual indulgence and self-mortification toward liberation and enlightenment. Here are some scriptural evidences of the Middle Way in the Pali Canon:

In the Majjhima Nikaya, the Buddha gave his monks a discourse on the "The Exposition of Non-Conflict" to teach the Middle Way. From MN 139, the Araṇavibhaṅga Sutta:

> *"Here, bhikkhus, **the Middle Way** discovered by the Tathagata avoids both these extremes; giving vision, giving knowledge, it leads to peace, to direct knowledge, to enlightenment, to Nibbana. It is a state without suffering...and it is the right way. Therefore this is a state without conflict."*[17]

And here, from Samyutta Nikaya: IV. The Book of the Six Sense Bases (Saḷāyatanavagga):

"There are, headman, these two extremes which should not be cultivated by one who has gone forth into homelessness: the pursuit of sensual happiness in sensual pleasures, which is low, vulgar, the way of worldlings, ignoble, unbeneficial; and the pursuit of self-mortification, which is painful, ignoble, unbeneficial.

Without veering towards either of these extremes, the **Tathagata has awakened to the Middle Way,** *which gives rise to vision, which gives rise to knowledge, which leads to peace, to direct knowledge, to enlightenment, to Nibbana. And* **what is that Middle Way awakened to by the Tathagata, which gives rise to vision . . . leads to Nibbana?**

It is this Noble Eightfold Path; *that is, right view . . . right concentration. This is that* **Middle Way** *awakened to by the Tathagata, which gives rise to vision, which gives rise to knowledge, which leads to peace, to direct knowledge, to enlightenment, to Nibbana."*[18]

From the Anguttara Nikaya: The Book of the Threes, Ways of Practice:

"Bhikkhus, there are these three ways of practice. What three? The coarse way of practice, the blistering way of practice, and the **Middle Way of practice.**

And what is the **Middle Way** *of practice? Here, a bhikkhu dwells contemplating the body in the body, ardent, clearly comprehending, mindful, having removed longing and dejection in regard to the world. He dwells contemplating feelings in feelings . . . mind in mind . . . phenomena in phenomena, ardent, clearly comprehending, mindful, having removed longing and dejection in regard to the world. This is called the Middle*

81

Way of practice. These, bhikkhus, are the three ways of practice."[19]

In fact, all of the Buddha's teachings as taught in the Pali Canon—ranging from Four Noble Truths, Eightfold Path, Dependent Co-arising—belong to the Law of the Middle Way for two reasons:

- First, all these teachings are contextualized according to the needs of the individual or situation (i.e. skillful means)
- Second, there exists a cause-and-effect relationship in the Dharma (e.g. Dependent Co-arising)

In summary, all the Buddha's teachings as documented in the Pali Canon are the Middle Way because the Dharma was delivered and taught in the context of a human world and in response to the suitability of individuals and circumstances. One of the most outstanding teachings of the Middle Way in the Theravada tradition is the Eightfold Path. Thus, the Middle Way is the truth of the Buddha's Skillful Means to benefit all living beings.

The Middle Way in the Practice of Dharma

In Theravada Buddhism, Dharma practice is all about our own efforts in accordance to the Law of Cause and Effect. In contrast, Mahayana Buddhism teaches a balance of self-efforts and divine support from Buddhas and bodhisattvas who help us achieve enlightenment quickly.

In Pure Land Buddhism, two methods of Self-Power (Jiriki 自力) and Other-Power (Tariki 他力) are equally important in the practice. In Section 4: The Practice of the Lotus Sutra, I will explain how the principle of the Middle Way applies in terms of the Lotus Sutra practice. It is a practical wisdom that, much as we try our best to be independent through self-efforts, we also need the support of others who can help us to quickly achieve our goals. Thus, the Middle-Way approach makes perfect sense in the Dharma practice.

2. The Middle Way Is the Truth of Law of Cause and Effect

Figure 9: A Chain

Another way of understanding the Middle Way is through the metaphor of a chain. A series of metal rings are linked to each other, which implies a "chain reaction" or a cause-and-effect relationship between two things. Doctrines such as Dependent Origination, Twelve-linked Chains of Causation, Ten Factors, and the Law of Cause and Effect that have the characteristics of the "chain reaction" belong to the Law of the Middle Way.

Doctrines of Middle Way in the Lotus Sutra

The Law of the Middle Way is found in the Lotus Sutra as well. It is expressed in the two doctrines:

- Ten Factors (Ten Suchness)
- Twelve-linked Chains of Causations (Dependent Origination)

Ten Factors

In Chapter 2: Expedient Methods of the Lotus Sutra, the Buddha expounded the Ten Factors or Ten Suchness (LS 2: 1.5) to explain the workings of the Law of Cause and Effect. Zhiyi uses the Ten Factors to derive his theory of Ichinen Sanzen.

> *O Shariputra! . . . The ultimate Law consists of such an appearance, such a nature, such an entity, such a force, such an action, such a cause, such an environment, such a result, such*

83

an effect, and such a coherent consistency from the beginning to the end. (LS 2: 1.5)

Ten Factors/Suchness	Meanings
#1 – Appearance 相	Visible, outer form
#2 – Nature 性	Invisible, inner disposition
#3 – Entity 体	The vessel that carries the appearance and nature
#4 – Force 力	Inherent power, strength, motivation, or energy to achieve something
#5 – Action 作	Visible movement or action when the force or energy is activated
#6 – Cause 因	The inherent tendencies or dispositions
#7 – Environment 缘	The external conditions that bring forth the inherent cause
#8 – Result 果	Latent or invisible outcome that spontaneously appears but is yet to be visibly manifested due to unfavourable conditions
#9 – Effect 报	Visible or manifested result that can be seen or evaluated, activated by external environment or condition
#10 – Consistency 本末 究竟等	All the nine factors are consistent from the beginning to the end

Figure 10: Meanings of the Ten Factors

As you can see, the Ten Factors are "linked" in a sense that the Law of Cause and Effect (factors 6 to 9) are woven into the Ten Factors, and that all the Ten Factors are consistent from beginning to end.

Twelve-Linked Chains of Causation

Twelve-linked Chains of Causation, otherwise known as Dependent Origination or Dependent Co-arising, is a doctrine of the Law of Cause and Effect.

Twelve-linked Chains of Causation delineate the process of eliminating rebirth. Rebirth begins with ignorance. Once the albatross of ignorance is eradicated, rebirth is ceased. Therefore wisdom, the opposite of ignorance, is the critical factor to uproot the causes of suffering arising in the endless cycles of rebirth. Here are the excerpts in the Lotus Sutra about the Twelve-linked Chains of Causation (LS 7: 4.2 – 4.3):

Ignorance causes action,
action causes consciousness,
consciousness causes name and form,
name and form cause the six sense organs,
the six sense organs cause contact,
contact causes sensation,
sensation causes loving desire,
loving desire causes attachment,
attachment causes existence,
existence causes birth,
birth causes old age, death, worry,
grief, anguish, and suffering.

If ignorance is ceased,
then action will be ceased.
If action is ceased,
then consciousness will be ceased.
If consciousness is ceased,
then name and form will be ceased.
If name and form are ceased,
then the six sense organs will be ceased.
If the six sense organs are ceased,
then contact will be ceased.
If contact is ceased,
then sensation will be ceased.
If sensation is ceased,

then loving desire will be ceased.
If loving desire is ceased,
then attachment will be ceased.
If attachment is ceased,
then birth will be ceased.
If birth is ceased,
then old age, death, worry,
grief, anguish, and suffering will be ceased.[20]

You will notice that the two teachings have something in common: they have "links" that connect from one factor to the next, or the "chains" of causes that denote the inter-dependent or cause-and-effect relationships among them.

In conclusion, the Middle Way is the Law of Cause and Effect or the Law of Karma. Doctrines such as Dependent Origination, Twelve-linked Chains of Causation, and Ten Factors belong to the Law of the Middle Way.

Application of the Law of Middle Way in Life

In a conditioned world of duality, the 'Goldilocks Principle' of the Middle Way is the True North to health and happiness. From the application perspective, the Middle Way means balance, oneness, unity, co-existence, harmony, inclusiveness, synthesis, unification of contradictions, integration of duality and dichotomy.

Everything in life hinges upon balance and oneness. To maintain good health, we need to have a balanced lifestyle comprising balanced diet, sufficient sleep, moderate exercise. The biological processes in our bodies are always in a delicate balance in order to have optimum health. A balance in our body, mind, and spirit is critical for us to experience health, peace, and happiness.

Life is always shades of grey. Suffering, inequality, and injustice are sometimes inevitable facts of life. There are many things that are beyond our control as they simply cannot be changed. Being born as men or women is one example. The biological differences of men and women mean that perfect equality cannot be completely achieved; we can only try to achieve equitable opportunities for men and women.

On the other hand, some Buddhists think that Buddhism is not about engaging in contemporary social issues. The Law of the Middle Way shows that we can balance individual salvation with social justice to benefit the wider community.

Buddhists can become socially engaged by becoming involved in politics and engaging with various social issues such as racial and gender equality, environmental protection, poverty, health and sanitation, as well as underprivileged children. Although the root of human suffering is in the mind and not the world, engaged Buddhists choose to take concrete actions to alleviate suffering in humans as a form of spiritual practice toward enlightenment. By standing up for social justice and fighting for human rights, they find meaning in their lives by working compassionately for the well-being of marginalized groups of people. Thus, engaged Buddhists have epitomized the spirit of humanity through their involvement in the muddy world of actual human suffering on Earth.

Conclusion

The Middle Way is the truth of the conditioned world of duality. All life forms are expressions of the Middle Way. From the application perspective, the Middle Way means balance, unity, and harmonious co-existence.

The Law of the Middle Way encompasses two truths: the truth of the Buddha's skillful means and the truth of Law of Cause and Effect. All the Buddha's teachings ranging from the Eightfold Path, Dependent Origination, Law of Cause and Effect, Twelve-linked Chains of Causations are expressions of the Middle Way.

In terms of the Dharma practice, the Middle Way applies. Both Jiriki (Self-Power) that entails self-efforts, and Tariki (Other-Power) that involves the divine support from Buddhas and bodhisattvas are necessary to achieve an optimum balance in the practice.

Truth #3: The Law of Buddhahood

The nature and the relationship of Buddhahood with Emptiness, Dependent Origination and the Middle Way are not clearly explained by Nagarjuna and Zhiyi. This is the missing element that needs more clarity.

Both Nagarjuna and Zhiyi perceived Emptiness to be equivalent to Dependent Origination and the Middle Way. My contemplation of Emptiness and Dependent Origination has shown otherwise. Emptiness and the Middle Way are two distinctive approaches to the Dharma. The Law of Emptiness is like water, and the Law of Middle Way is like oil; they cannot be mixed together.

The Law of Buddhahood is Oneness of the Law of Emptiness and the Law of Middle Way

In the previous section, we learned about the compassion aspect of the Buddha and the Dharma through the Three Gifts, in which the Buddha gives his Dharma of One Buddha-Vehicle and his merits generously to support his disciples' quick attainment.

In this section, you will understand about the wisdom aspect of the Law of Buddhahood through its relationship with the Law of Emptiness and the Law of Middle Way. The Law of Buddhahood is oneness of the Law of Emptiness and the Law of Middle Way as shown in the following equation:

> **Law of Buddhahood = Law of Emptiness + Law of Middle Way**

Although the Law of Emptiness and the Law of Middle Way are like water and oil, the Law of Buddhahood is a powerful transformational agent that enables the mixing of water and oil into one.

In the Lotus Sutra, Chapter 2 represents the Law of the Middle Way (i.e. Expedient Methods) and Chapter 16 represents the Law of Emptiness (i.e. Eternal Lifespan of a Dharmakaya Buddha). The essence of the Lotus Sutra is the Dharma of Buddhahood that integrates the Law of Middle Way (Chapter 2) and the Law of Emptiness (Chapter 16).

The Law of Buddhahood is the All-Inclusive Teaching

As mentioned in Section 2: Gift of the Law, there are six different types of "One" found in the Lotus Sutra. For the purpose of illustrating the Law of Buddhahood as the unity of Law of Emptiness and Law of Middle Way, I will explain the meaning of "All" (一切).

The Chinese term "Yi Qie" (一切) means "All and Everything." The Buddha declared that the Lotus Sutra contains "All" his teachings and that it has the power to cure all types of sufferings. Here are the two quotes:

The Lotus Sutra Contains All the Buddha's Teachings

> *In essence, I have revealed and expounded* ***all*** *the teachings of Tathagata,* ***all*** *the effortless divine powers of Tathagata,* ***all*** *the Secret Treasuries of Tathagata, and* ***all*** *the profound historical events of Tathagatas in the Lotus Sutra. Therefore, after the parinirvana of Tathagata, all of you shall single-mindedly practice the Law by accepting, embracing, reading, reciting, explaining, preaching, copying, and transcribing the Lotus Sutra. (LS 21: 1.8)*

The Lotus Sutra is Capable of Saving All Living Beings from All Sufferings

> *The Lotus Sutra is able to save **all** living beings. The Lotus Sutra is able to deliver **all** living beings from excruciating pains and bitter suffering. The Lotus Sutra is able to bring abundant benefits and blessings to **all** living beings, fulfilling their desires, hopes, and dreams. Just as the clear and cooling pool is able to quench thirst….. so is the Lotus Sutra; it is able to end **all** sorts of suffering, illnesses, and pains of living beings by breaking the bondage of birth and death. (LS 23: 2.9-2.10)*

The Law of Buddhahood is special because it has the all-encompassing power to lead all living beings to enlightenment in a creative and empowering manner. Metaphorically speaking, the Law of Buddhahood is *both* the empty receptacle *and* the objects inside the receptacle. In other words, the Law of Buddhahood is akin to the white light exuding from the receptacle and the objects. Just as the white light exhibits wave-particle duality under different conditions, the Law of Buddhahood expresses both the Law of Emptiness and Law of Middle Way in response to different circumstances.

The Law of Buddhahood is like the Buddha having the three bodies (Trikaya): Nirmanakaya (Manifested Physical Body), Sambhogakaya (Reward/Enjoyment Body), and Dharmakaya (Truth Body). Under different conditions, the Buddha will manifest his body in different ways.

The Law of Emptiness is the truth of an unconditional world and the Law of Middle Way is the truth of a conditioned world. Both of them are distinctive, independent, and mutually exclusive; the Law of Emptiness is not identical with the Law of the Middle Way. This means that the Law of Emptiness is not the Dependent Origination (teaching of the Middle Way) as previously taught by Nagarjuna.

The Law of Emptiness ≠ The Law of Middle Way

However, the Law of Emptiness is synonymous to the Law of Buddhahood because both abide in the unconditional world and they do *not* dependently co-arise in response to causes and conditions, unlike the doctrine of Dependent Origination and Law of Cause and Effect. The true nature of the Law of Buddhahood is the Law of Emptiness because the Law of Emptiness encapsulates the qualities of Purity, Eternity, True Self, and Bliss that are the Four Virtues of Dharmakaya Buddha. The Law of Emptiness also means that the realm of Buddhahood is an inconceivable world of infinite creativity and boundless possibilities.

However, when conditions arise, the Dharmakaya Buddha becomes the Nirmanakaya Buddha when the Buddha chooses to be reborn as a human to teach the Dharma just like Shakyamuni Buddha did. The Nirmanakaya Buddha is an expression of the Law of the Middle Way for two reasons:

1) this manifested Buddha is dependently co-arisen due to causes and conditions, and
2) he will "appear" to pass on by entering Nirvana, which is skillful means in action.

The Law of Buddhahood, being the integration and oneness of the Law of Emptiness and the Law of the Middle Way, is significant for the following reasons:

1) We, as entities of the Law of the Middle Way, are already endowed with the potential (i.e. Buddha-nature) to become a Buddha. All we need to do is to awaken it.
2) We can attain Buddhahood by meditating upon the Law of Emptiness. Meditation upon the Law of Emptiness is nothing new: many Mahayana sutras (e.g. Prajnaparamita Sutras) teach about meditation upon Emptiness, and it is one of the core practices of Tibetan Buddhism as well.

3) We can also attain Buddhahood by practicing the teachings in early Buddhism (e.g. the Pali Canon) such as the Four Noble Truths and Eightfold Path which belong to the Law of the Middle Way.

Of course, we can also attain Buddhahood by meditating upon and practicing the Law of Buddhahood, such as in the Lotus Sutra.

Theory of Mutual Possession in the Law of Buddhahood

Zhiyi's Ichinen Sanzen is understood as the world of Buddhahood containing the rest of the nine worlds below (from Hell to Bodhisattva); but so too does the world of Hell contain the rest of the nine worlds above it (Hungry Spirits to Buddhahood). This is the theory of the "mutual possession of the Ten Worlds," which means that life at any given moment is not fixed but can manifest any of Ten Worlds. Thus, even though we are humans, we can manifest either Hell or Buddhahood, depending on our thoughts, speech, and actions.

Since the Law of Buddhahood is the unification of the Law of Emptiness and the Law of Middle Way, this means that the world of Buddhahood can manifest either the True Self (Law of Emptiness) or the Expedient Self (Law of Middle Way). In a sense, the Law of Buddhahood reflects the mutual possession of ultimate reality and expedient reality depending on various conditions. For instance, the ultimate truth of a Buddha is that of Dharmakaya (Law of Emptiness), but he can manifest himself as Nirmanakaya or Sambhogakaya (Law of Middle Way) in response to external conditions. Therefore, we as humans are beings of the Middle Way, but we can also manifest characteristics identical to the state of Buddhahood (Law of Emptiness).

On the other hand, many people subscribe to the view that the impermanent phenomena that are constantly changing are a reflection of Emptiness.[21] I beg to differ. Why? Because Emptiness means eternity, and it also means nothing changes. Based on the theory of the Law of Buddhahood—being the integration of the Law of Emptiness and the Law of the Middle Way—this shows that the ephemeral and fluid characteristic of the phenomena is actually the expression of the Middle Way subsumed in the Law of Buddhahood. In other words, all the characteristics and expressions in a conditioned—as well as non-conditioned world—are splendid manifestations of the Law of Buddhahood.

In summary, the Law of Buddhahood can be understood as the mutual possession of the ultimate truth and expedient reality, which is similar to the theory of Ichinen Sanzen in terms of mutual possession of the Ten Worlds. This denotes that we as humans already possess the world of Buddhahood within us. By meditating upon the natures of the Law of Emptiness—Infinity, Eternity, and Purity—we can grasp the essence of Buddhahood in terms of the Four Virtues of True Self, Eternity, Purity, and Happiness. This also explains why most Mahayana sutras teach the method of meditating upon the Law of Emptiness as a means to achieving Buddhahood.

Buddhahood = Journey + Destination

Some of you may be wondering: Is Buddhahood a goal to be attained? Or is Buddhahood a voyage to be experienced? The truth is, Buddhahood is as much a destination to arrive as it is a journey to be experienced.

93

The doctrine of Original Enlightenment, or *hongaku*,[22] holds the view that, since all living beings have the Buddha-nature, they are already enlightened in some way just as they are. Dao Sheng, who wrote the first commentary of the Lotus Sutra, postulated the view of "sudden enlightenment." Master Huineng also taught in the Platform Sutra[23] that by seeing our original nature, we can achieve "sudden enlightenment" as opposed to gradual attainment of "acquired enlightenment" (shikaku). This means that enlightenment is an experience to be realized in our ordinary lives, because we are already inherently endowed with enlightenment.

In Chapter 12, the dragon girl showed her skeptics who did not believe that a woman could3 become a Buddha by quickly transforming herself into a man and becoming a Buddha literally in an instant, before reverting to her old self as a dragon girl. Her transformation is meant to show people that the Lotus Sutra enables one to quickly, not immediately, attain Buddhahood. The so called "sudden enlightenment" is just an experience, not the ultimate destination.

The Law of Buddhahood helps us understand that although we dwell in a human body, we can experience Buddhahood through our daily lives as a human. Just like a Zen master who experiences *satori* or "sudden enlightenment" by hearing a bird's chirping or the roll of thunder, we can experience moments of awakening through the most mundane, insignificant, and ordinary human experiences.

By taking the Middle Way as our means to understand enlightenment, Buddhahood is as much an ultimate destination to be accomplished as it is a journey to be experienced.

Application of the Law of Buddhahood in Life

Buddhahood means empowerment and transformation toward spiritual perfection. It gives us hope when we know that we have the power within us to transform our lives. If we recognize the Eternal Buddha within us, we can galvanize the vast reservoir of our highest potential to overcome all obstacles and accomplish the Mission Impossible.

Many Zen Buddhist monks attained spontaneous awakening and enlightenment through perceiving the perfection in the most mundane aspects of life and nature at that particular moment: a cup of steaming tea, swirling clouds, a flowing river, chirping birds, etc. Buddhahood is the supreme expression of the perfection inherent in nature and life.

I have heard innumerable personal experiences and testimonials from people achieving medical miracles and personal transformations by chanting the daimoku with hope and faith. One real-life example is the experience of John Wong,[24] who overcame his paralysis by regenerating his own neurons through chanting and a personal conviction of his innate power. It was a medical miracle because neurons, once destroyed, cannot be regenerated—but he did it. This is a testament writ large of empowerment in action.

Once we are awakened to the Law of Buddhahood that is pervasive in all sentient and non-sentient beings, we will not be shackled by fear and anxiety as we go through the vicissitudes of life. Knowing that we have the Eternal Buddha inside of us, coupled with the divine protection of all the Buddhas and bodhisattvas, we are empowered to transform any poison into medicine to live a meaningful life, contributing to the happiness of humanity.

Conclusion

The Law of Buddhahood is oneness of the Law of Emptiness and the Law of Middle Way, just like the white light exhibiting wave-particle duality.

While the Law of Emptiness and the Law of Middle Way are mutually exclusive, the true essence of the Law of Buddhahood is the Law of Emptiness. It is only under a specific condition that the Law of Buddhahood expresses itself as the Law of the Middle Way.

The significance of the Law of Buddhahood is that we, as entities of the Law of the Middle Way, are already endowed with the potential to become a Buddha. Regardless of whether we meditate or practice the Law of Emptiness, Law of Middle Way, or the Law of Buddhahood, we are certain to attain Buddhahood.

Section 3:

The Practice of the Lotus Sutra

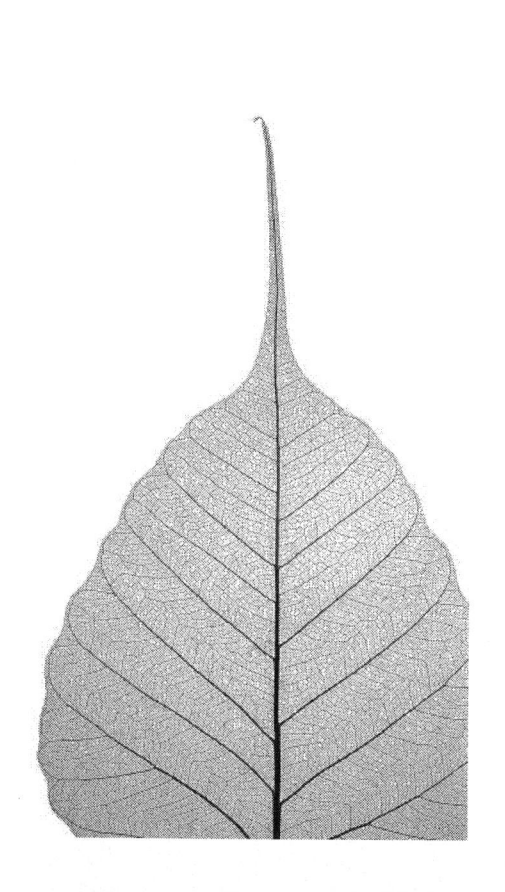

Different Styles of Practice

The truth is, you do not need to practice the Lotus Sutra to attain Buddhahood, because all types of expedient practices such as practicing loving-kindness and compassion (LS 2: 5.39), the Six Paramitas (LS 2: 5.38), creating Buddha's images (LS 2: 5.43), giving music as offerings to the Buddha (LS 2: 5.49) will result in attaining Buddhahood. Nevertheless, the wonderful method of the practice of the Lotus Sutra will enable you to quickly accomplish unsurpassed enlightenment.

The Lotus Sutra is interpreted differently by different Buddhist masters, which results in diverse ways of practice. There are three notable Buddhist masters who wrote commentaries on the Lotus Sutra: Zhu Dao Sheng, Zhiyi, and Nichiren. Dao Sheng promulgated the philosophy of immediate, sudden, or spontaneous attainment of Buddhahood,[1] which is adopted by Zen Buddhism in its core practice. He also affirmed that all people, including the *icchantikas* (people of incorrigible disbelief), can attain Buddhahood. However, he concluded that Confucian and Buddhist philosophy are compatible and identical in their goals, which might not be entirely accurate.[2]

As for Zhiyi, although he identified the Lotus Sutra as the ultimate teaching of the Buddha, he taught his disciples the meditation upon Amitabha Buddha and the chanting of "Namu Amitabha Buddha" in *Great Concentration and Insight*.[3] He derived this practice based on the Pratyutpanna Samadhi Sutra, a Amitabha-based meditation sutra.[4]

Thus, it is not surprising that while Nichiren, Dogen, and Honen studied Zhiyi's philosophies at Tendai temples, Honen subsequently established a Pure Land school that focuses on the practice of the Amitabha Buddha while Dogen established the Zen school. Only Nichiren perceived the Lotus Sutra as the ultimate teaching to be widely propagated for the benefit of humanity.

Nichiren established the chanting of the title of the Lotus Sutra, also known as the daimoku of Nam Myoho Renge Kyo, as the essential practice. He taught that the recitation of any of the 28 chapters, which includes Chapter 2 and Chapter 16, is merely a supplementary practice.[5]

The Three One-Heart Methods

When it comes to the practice of Buddhism in general, and the Lotus Sutra in particular, there is no hard and fast rule as to which one is the "true" or "correct" practice; it is all dependent on the individual's preferences.

The practice of the Lotus Sutra as prescribed by Shakyamuni Buddha is different from the methods created by both Zhiyi and Nichiren. Because the Lotus Sutra is infused with the life and divine powers of the Buddha, you will notice later that the practice of the Lotus Sutra focuses predominantly on the scripture. This means that all you need is The Book.

In fact, the Buddha wants us to understand that, while having a teacher in physical form can be useful especially for beginners, the sutra as the primary source is the most reliable teacher, especially for advanced practitioners, and you do not need a physical teacher. This scriptural-focus practice is regarded as the "Special Method" because you are literally practicing the Triple Refuge, developing bodhicitta (aspiration for enlightenment) and polishing the samadhi (single-pointed concentration) just by single-mindedly practicing the Lotus Sutra.

In Section 1: Insights of the Lotus Sutra, I mentioned six types of "one" found in the Lotus Sutra. With respect to the practice, I am going to focus on the Chinese character of "Yi Xin" （一心）, which means "one heart," "single-mindedly," or "wholeheartedly."

The spirit of practicing the Lotus Sutra is "single-mindedness." By concentrating upon just the One Dharma of Buddhahood, we are developing samadhi in our minds. Let us find out what are the Three One-Heart Methods:

- Practice the Lotus Sutra
- Propagate the Lotus Sutra
- Be mindful of Bodhisattva Avalokitesvara

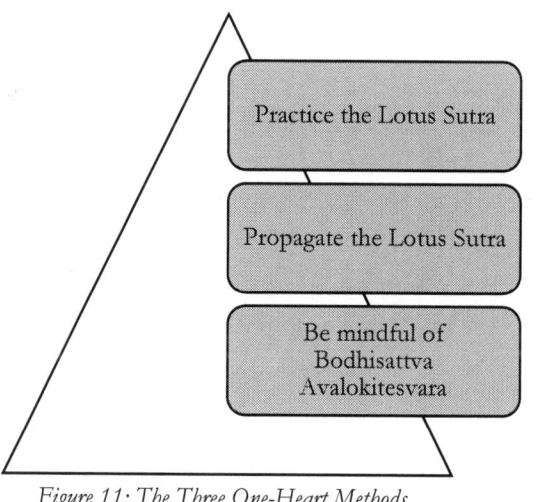

Figure 11: The Three One-Heart Methods

1. Practice the Lotus Sutra

The Lotus Sutra is the embodiment of Buddhahood. This is because it encapsulates the Dharmakaya of the Eternal Buddha within the sutra itself. Most Mahayana sutras present three ways to attain Buddhahood: attain samadhi, meditate upon emptiness, or recite the sutras.[6] The Lotus Sutra belongs to the third method, which focuses on the scripture.

> *In essence, I have revealed and expounded all the teachings of Tathagata, all the effortless divine powers of Tathagata, all the Secret Treasuries of Tathagata, and all the profound historical events of Tathagata in the Lotus Sutra. Therefore, after the parinirvana of Tathagata, all of you shall* **single-mindedly practice the Law by accepting, embracing, reading, reciting, explaining, preaching, copying, and transcribing the Lotus Sutra.** *(LS 21: 1.8)*

In Chapter 21, the Buddha expounded the "8+1 Methods" to practice the Lotus Sutra:

- accept (受)
- embrace (持)
- read (读)
- recite (诵)
- explain (解)
- preach (说)
- copy (书)
- transcribe (写)
- practice mindfulness (正忆念)

#1 - Accept

Accept the Law of Buddhahood with Faith

To accept means to receive the Buddha-Dharma wholeheartedly, with an open mind and a joyous heart. Faith is the key to embracing the Dharma. Here are some of the scriptural evidences on accepting the Buddha's teaching with joy, faith, and understanding:

> *"O Shariputra! You should wholeheartedly accept and embrace the words of the Buddha with faith and understanding. The words of all Buddha-Tathagata are the truth: there are no alternative Vehicles, only the One Buddha-Vehicle." (LS 2: 4.15)*

> *"O Ajita! If there are virtuous men and women who are able to have profound faith and understanding upon hearing of my eternal lifespan, then it means that they have already seen the Buddha constantly preaching the Law amidst the great bodhisattvas and the community of shravakas at Eagle Peak." (LS 17: 3.2)*

> *"Again, after the parinirvana of Tathagata, if there are people who respond with spontaneous joy upon hearing the Lotus Sutra, instead of slandering it, then you should know that this is a sign of their profound faith and understanding. How much more so of those people who read, recite, accept, and embrace the Lotus Sutra! Such people are actually carrying the Tathagata on the crowns of their heads!" (LS 17: 3.3)*

> *"...By applying the power of expedient methods, her two sons had skillfully transformed their father, leading him to have faith and understanding as well as to experience joy in the Buddha-Law." (LS 27: 2.4)*

#2 - Embrace

Practice the Lotus Sutra with Commitment

To embrace means to hold it closely without giving up easily. It indicates the strength of commitment, tenacity, resilience, and perseverance in the practice. The real victory in the practice of Buddhism is whether we have the power of faith and fortitude to sustain our practice toward the final journey of our lives.

#3 - Read

Read the Lotus Sutra

Reading the Lotus Sutra is the practice that empowers us with the wisdom of the Dharma of Anuttara Samyak Sambodhi. The act of studying the sutra embodies the spirit of learning that helps us to gain greater understanding and appreciation of the Dharma, which in turn contributes to strengthening our faith in the practice. Besides, reading the sutra is the only and the most reliable way to receive the teachings directly from Shakyamuni Buddha himself. This helps us to connect our ordinary minds with the enlightened minds of the Buddha.

#4 - Recite

Recite the Lotus Sutra

To recite means "to repeat aloud from memory through intoning or chanting." Chanting is the core practice of Nichiren Buddhism. Contrary to the common belief and popular practice of seated meditation in Western Buddhism, for centuries the predominant Buddhist practice entailed chanting or reciting the various Mahayana sutras, especially from the Mahayana traditions in China, Korea, and Japan.[7] Chanting does not have to be monotonous; it can be wonderfully rhythmic and melodious, just like music. Thus, singing the sutras can be a splendid method of recitation that elicits the joy of Dharma.

#5 - Understand

Understand the Law of Buddhahood

There are many ways to equip ourselves with the Buddha's teachings. We can read books written by Buddhist masters or experienced Buddhist practitioners, attend Dharma talks or lectures, or even associate with Dharma friends to educate ourselves in the knowledge and wisdom of the Buddha-Dharma.

Nevertheless, the most reliable and optimum way to learn about Buddhism in general, or the Lotus Sutra in particular, is to read the primary source as presented in the sutras. Thanks to the efforts of numerous Buddhist organizations, English translations are increasingly available and accessible for a Western audience.

For beginners, reading the Lotus Sutra directly without any background knowledge will be a challenging experience. For a start, you can read the commentaries on the Lotus Sutra by Buddhist masters such as Master Hsuan Hua, Zhiyi, or Nichiren. Once you have some basic understanding, it is highly recommended for you to read the Lotus Sutra on your own so that you can perceive fresh concepts not previously discovered by any previous Buddhist masters.

#6 - Explain

Explain to Others

As mentioned in Dhammapada 354, the gift of Dharma exceeds all gifts.[8] Sharing Buddhism with others is an act of profound generosity and compassion. By sharing the Dharma with your family and friends, you help them form a spiritual connection with the Buddha and his teachings.

To be able to share the Lotus Sutra confidently and joyously, we need to be empowered by educating ourselves through reading and learning the Lotus Sutra consistently. Besides, we also need to experience the benefits arising from the practice itself so that we have personal testimonials to joyously share the actual proof of our Buddhist practice.

105

#7 - Copy

Copy the Lotus Sutra

Copying means transcribing the Lotus Sutra word by word. Doing a translation of the Lotus Sutra is a form of transcribing the words from one language to another.

An alternative way of copying the Lotus Sutra is by writing calligraphy. It is a popular practice in East Asian cultures to write the Chinese characters of the sutra via a calligraphic brush and ink. For many people, calligraphy as a Dharma practice is a therapeutic experience that brings meditative calm to the scattered brain. Give it a try!

#8 - Write

Write about the Lotus Sutra

Writing about the Lotus Sutra means producing written works related to the Lotus Sutra. A book, or any written work, is a powerful way to preserve the wisdom of a Buddhist practitioner who may inspire us to live with courage and hope through the Buddha's teachings. Some examples include:

- writing commentaries or treatises about the Lotus Sutra,
- sharing personal experience or testimonials about the practice through written words,
- or publishing books, articles, theses, or blog posts related to the Lotus Sutra.

#9 – Right Mindfulness

Have the Right Mindfulness

Apart from the eight methods mentioned above, there is a ninth method documented in Chapter 28. Having right mindfulness means having the ability to memorize and remember the words of the Buddha. By concentrating upon the Buddha's words, we will align our minds to the enlightened mind of the Buddha. This is a type of meditation practice to awaken and polish our innate Buddhahood:

> *"O Universal Worthy! If there are people who are able to accept, embrace, read, and recite the Lotus Sutra, **memorize it correctly,** and practice the sutra as it is taught, you should know that these people have already seen Shakyamuni Buddha. It is as though they have heard the Lotus Sutra directly from the mouth of Shakyamuni Buddha. You should know that these people have given offerings to Shakyamuni Buddha. You should know that these people have been praised 'Excellent!' by Shakyamuni Buddha. You should know that these people have been patted on the head by Shakyamuni Buddha. You should know that these people have been covered in the robes of Shakyamuni Buddha." (LS 28: 2.2)*

2. Propagate the Lotus Sutra

Practicing the Lotus Sutra goes beyond just self-practice; spreading the Law is the practice to benefit others. Propagating the Lotus Sutra is the mission of all Buddha's disciples. If we do not actively share Buddhism, we will not be able to bring benefits to people who sincerely wish to transform their lives to become happy through the Buddha's teachings, not to mention the long-term sustainability of the Dharma, which could be at stake.

In Chapter 22: Entrustment, the Buddha entrusts his disciples to Law to propagate the Law of Anuttara Samyak Sambodhi single-mindedly and wholeheartedly for the benefits of others:

> *At that time, Shakyamuni Buddha rose from his Dharma seat and then displayed his great divine powers by using his right hand to touch the crowns of immeasurable bodhisattvas-mahasattvas. After which, he proceeded to make the declaration: "For immeasurable hundreds of thousands of millions of billions of asamkhya kalpas, I have practiced this Law of Supreme Perfect Enlightenment that is rare and difficult to attain. Now, I have entrusted the Law to you. You must **wholeheartedly** focus on widely propagating the Law*

> *so as to bring increased benefits, blessings, and prosperity for all." (LS 22: 1.1)*

In a nutshell, spreading the Dharma of Buddhahood is akin to fulfilling the vows of a great bodhisattva.

Importance in Conversion

Some people perceive that the Buddhist practice is not about converting others to the Buddhist faith. This is far from truth. Buddhism is as much about converting people as the Abrahamic religions. If we take a leaf out of Buddha's book in terms of building a Sangha, we will understand the importance of conversion for the long-term survival and sustainability of Buddhism. The actions of Shakyamuni Buddha are the solid proof of the importance of conversion:

First Five Disciples

Immediately after Shakyamuni Buddha had attained enlightenment, he set out to teach his Dharma to the first five disciples—Kondanna, Bhaddiya, Vappa, Mahanama and Assaji—at Sarnath without delay. This very action of Shakyamuni Buddha is a testament of his unwavering commitment to the propagation of Dharma.

The Kashyapa Brothers

The Kashyapa brothers—Uruvilva-Kashyapa, Gaya-Kashyapa, Nadi-Kashyapa—were the Buddha's early converts. As powerful Brahman ascetics who practiced the fire worship, the three brothers converted to Shakyamuni's teachings after witnessing the divine powers of the Buddha. All of their 1,000 devotees followed the three brothers in joining the order of the Sangha.

Sundara-Nanda

Sundara-Nanda was the half-brother of Shakyamuni Buddha. He had little interest in the Dharma, for he loved his wife more than anything else. After joining the Sangha, his heart was not anchored upon practicing the Dharma. The Buddha stepped in and used his divine powers as skillful means to show Sundara-Nanda the karmic results of being born in heaven and hell. After witnessing the benefits of being reborn in the heaven, Sundara-Nanda practiced the Dharma assiduously and subsequently attained arhatship.

Conversion is critical in the long-term sustainability of a wonderful philosophy that can benefit people. From a positive viewpoint, think of conversion as getting "buy-in" or "acceptance" due to radical change of hearts.

Modern Ways of Propagating Buddhism and the Lotus Sutra

Let us review a few methods used by Buddhist teachers in the past and present to propagate the Lotus Sutra:

Analytical Refutation

Analytical refutation is a method that converts other through scholastic debate. This is the predominant method used by disciples of Tiantai Buddhism as well as Nichiren himself to win over new converts.

Thus, it is not surprising to find modern Nichiren sects adopting similar mindset by "righteously refuting" other Nichiren sects in order to justify the "superiority" of their doctrines and sects. Some aspects of refutation include priesthood authority, legitimate power of Dai-Gohonzon, perceived "right" methods of donation, etc.

The downside to this method is its exclusivist attitude at best, or its intolerant behavior toward different Buddhist faiths at worst. The Buddha's teaching of skillful means reminds us to recognize the diverse spiritual needs of others by honoring diversity and accepting different styles of practices respectfully and non-judgmentally. In a pluralistic society that cherishes harmonious co-existence, being inclusive and embracing other Buddhist sects go a long way in fostering peace within the Sangha.

Engaged or Humanistic Buddhism

Many modern Buddhist schools such as Fo Guang Shan, Thich Nhat Hanh's Plum Village, Tzu Chi Charitable Foundation, and Soka Gakkai International practice a style of Buddhism known as Engaged Buddhism or Humanistic Buddhism.

This style of Buddhist practice integrates Buddhist philosophy into daily life by engaging in secular activities such as world peace through inter-faith dialogues, environmental activism, social justice, disaster and humanitarian efforts, as well as cultural and educational activities. In this way, Buddhist practice becomes relevant and practical in daily modern life, which is instrumental in attracting people to adopt Buddhism.

Actual Proof of the Practice

The most powerful way to share Buddhism is the actual proof of the practice. If you experience a change in your life as a result of your Buddhist practice, you will have the confidence to joyously share Buddhism with your family and friends. People who are inspired by your transformation will be motivated to embrace Buddhism as well.

Ultimately, the practice of Buddhism and the Lotus Sutra is to become happy. We want to develop courage and life force to transform our lives by overcoming all challenges so that we can live happy and peaceful lives.

3. Be Mindful of Bodhisattva Avalokitesvara

Bodhisattva Avalokitesvara, the epitome of profound compassion, is the most beloved and popular bodhisattva in East Asian Buddhism, especially in Chinese Buddhism. For centuries, *Chapter 25: Universal Gateway of Bodhisattva Avalokitesvara* became an independent sutra on its own in Chinese Buddhism due to the popularity of Bodhisattva Avalokitesvara.

This bodhisattva has various names in different cultures and traditions: Guan Yin in Chinese Buddhism, Chenrezig in Tibetan Buddhism, or Kannon in Japanese Buddhism. Many Buddhists express their devotion to Bodhisattva Avalokitesvara by either intoning "Namo Guan Shi Yin Pu Sa," (meaning "Devotion to Bodhisattva Avalokitesvara") or chant his mantra of "Om Mani Padme Hum" (meaning "Jewel in the Lotus").

Compassion has the power to protect us and avert disasters. The purpose of practicing the mindfulness of Bodhisattva Avalokitesvara is to cultivate the virtue of compassion and benevolence within our hearts. In Chapter 25, the Buddha taught his disciples to be mindful of the name of Bodhisattva Avalokitesvara in times of adversity for divine salvation (LS 25: 1.2), as well as paying respect to Bodhisattva Avalokitesvara (LS 25: 1.17) through giving offerings. It is interesting to note that, in Tiantai and Nichiren Buddhism, Bodhisattva Avalokitesvara has somehow eclipsed into oblivion to the point of "non-existence." Let us review the scriptural evidence about the mindfulness practice with respect to Bodhisattva Avalokitesvara:

> *The Buddha replied to Bodhisattva Infinite Intention: "My virtuous son! Suppose there are immeasurable hundreds of thousands of millions of billions of living beings who are suffering from pain and grief. If they hear the name Bodhisattva Avalokitesvara and call his name* **wholeheartedly with a focused mind***, then Bodhisattva Avalokitesvara will*

immediately respond to their voices and liberate them from suffering." (LS 25: 1.2)

"O Infinite Intention! This Bodhisattva Avalokitesvara has accomplished merits by transforming into various forms and traveling throughout the lands to save living beings. Hence, all of you should **wholeheartedly give offerings to Bodhisattva Avalokitesvara.** *" (LS 25: 1.17)*

Attaining Buddhahood through Bodhisattva Avalokitesvara

Paying homage to Bodhisattva Avalokitesvara is a practice that enables one to eventually attain Buddhahood. In Chapter 10 of the Lotus Sutra, the Buddha reassured his disciples that "whoever experiences a momentary joy upon any one phrase of the Lotus Sutra" (which includes Chapter 25 on Bodhisattva Avalokitesvara) will surely attain Buddhahood:

> *At that time, the Bhagavat addressed eighty thousand great leaders through Bodhisattva Medicine King: "O Medicine King! As you can see in this great assembly of immeasurable living beings——heavenly gods, dragons kings, yakshas, gandharvas, asuras...***anyone who experiences a momentary joy upon hearing one stanza or even one phrase of the Lotus Sutra in the presence of the Buddha, I shall bestow a prophecy that all of them will surely attain Supreme Perfect Enlightenment.'** *(LS 10: 1.1)*

Moreover, worshipping Bodhisattva Avalokitesvara is equivalent to giving offerings to Shakyamuni Buddha and Abundant Treasures Tathagata, as evidenced from the action of Bodhisattva Avalokitesvara who offered the necklace he received from Bodhisattva Infinite Intention to Shakyamuni Buddha and Abundant Treasures Buddha:

Bodhisattva Avalokitesvara accepted the necklace at once because of his compassion for the four groups, heavenly gods, dragons, humans, non-human beings, and the rest. Splitting the necklace into two, he presented one to Shakyamuni Buddha and the other one to the pagoda of Abundant Treasures Buddha. (LS 25: 1.22)

Four Fascinating Scriptural Facts about Bodhisattva Avalokitesvara

We can learn more about Bodhisattva Avalokitesvara in many Mahayana sutras. The following scriptural quotes show that Bodhisattva Avalokitesvara had already become a Buddha, known as *True Dharma Bright Tathagata*, when Shakyamuni was still a bodhisattva practicing asceticism. In fact, he was a teacher guiding Shakyamuni to attain Buddhahood.

Currently, Bodhisattva Avalokitesvara is an acolyte of Amitabha Buddha in the Western Pure Land, and he will become a Buddha with the name *King of Universal Light and Mountainous Merits Tathagata* after the parinirvana of Amitabha Buddha.

#1 – Guan Yin has already attained Buddhahood

In *The Sutra of Great Compassionate Heart Dharani of Bodhisattva Avalokitesvara with Thousand Hands and Thousand Eyes Sutra* (千手千眼 观世音菩萨大悲心陀罗尼), Bodhisattva Avalokitesvara has already attained Buddhahood eons ago and his Buddha's name is *True Dharma Bright Tathagata*:

Bodhisattva Avalokitesvara has inconceivable divine powers. He had already attained Buddhahood in the immeasurable kalpas ago and his name is True Dharma Bright Tathagata. By virtue of his power of great compassion and vows to bring peace and happiness for the living beings, he manifests himself as a bodhisattva.[9]

#2 – Bodhisattva Avalokitesvara was the teacher of Shakyamuni Buddha

In *The Sutra of the Secret Dharma of Thousand Bright Eyes Bodhisattva Avalokitesvara* (千光眼观自在菩萨秘密法经), Shakyamuni Buddha revealed that Bodhisattva Avalokitesvara was already a Buddha named *True Dharma Bright Tathagata* who taught and transformed beings into Buddhas in the Universe:

> *Before I attained Buddhahood, Guan Yin was a Buddha named True Dharma Bright Tathagata. At that time, I was a disciple practicing asceticism. All Tathagatas in the ten directions were taught and transformed by Bodhisattva Avalokitesvara.*[10]

#3 – Bodhisattva Avalokitesvara is the acolyte of Amitabha Buddha

In *The Sutra on the Meditation of the Infinite Life Buddha* (观无量寿经), one of the three Pure Land sutras, Shakyamuni Buddha revealed Bodhisattva Avalokitesvara and Bodhisattva Mahasthamaprapta as the acolytes of Amitabha Buddha.

> *The Infinite Life Buddha suspends in mid-air. Bodhisattva Avalokitesvara and Bodhisattva Mahasthamaprapta are his great acolytes supporting him on his left and right.*[11]

#4 – Bodhisattva Avalokitesvara will become a Buddha again after parinirvana of Amitabha Buddha

In *The Bestowal of Prophecy to Bodhisattva Avalokitesvara Sutra* (观世音菩萨授记经), Shakyamuni Buddha revealed that after the parinirvana of Amitabha Buddha, Bodhisattva Avalokitesvara will become a Buddha known as *King of Universal Light and Mountainous Merits Tathagata*.

> *After the extinction of the True Dharma of Amitabha Buddha, right after the stroke of midnight, Bodhisattva Avalokitesvara will sit in the lotus position under the seven-jewelled bodhi tree and achieve Supreme Perfect Enlightenment. His name will be known as King of Universal Light and Mountainous Merits Tathagata.[12]*

In conclusion, these four little-known but fascinating scriptural facts of Bodhisattva Avalokitesvara are testaments of his immeasurable compassion, wisdom, and divine powers for the salvation and happiness of all living beings. By studying Chapter 25 and practicing mindfulness of Bodhisattva Avalokitesvara, we can purify our lives and foster profound compassion for ourselves and others.

Salvation through Faith and Grace

While Method #1 (Practice the Lotus Sutra) and Method #2 (Propagate the Lotus Sutra) are two methods of attaining Buddhahood through personal efforts, Method #3 (Be Mindful of Bodhisattva Avalokitesvara) is a method of salvation through divine grace of Bodhisattva Avalokitesvara.

When it comes to salvation through divine grace, one may be reminded of practices of Christianity or the Pure Land's practice of relying upon Amitabha Buddha for rebirth in the Pure Land.[13]

Nevertheless, although the Lotus Sutra does not teach the practice of meditation upon Amitabha Buddha, the practice of having faith in and keeping mindful of Bodhisattva Avalokitesvara is intimately associated with the Pure Land practice. The salvation through faith and grace recognizes the existence of a transcendental world beyond the realm of human. It is a testament that we are not just humans, but rather spiritual beings who can tap into the immensely creative and limitless power of the Universe to create boundless possibilities in life.

Conclusion

When it comes to the Dharma practice, we need to embrace the virtue of single-mindedness or wholeheartedness. Thus, the Three One-Heart Methods is a comprehensive practice taught by the Buddha to practice the Lotus Sutra:

Method #1: Practice the Lotus Sutra through the 8+1 Methods: accept, embrace, read, recite, understand, explain, copy, write, and have right mindfulness.

Method #2: Propagate the Lotus Sutra to benefit all sentient beings as well as to preserve the Dharma.

Method #3: Be mindful of Bodhisattva Avalokitesvara to receive divine protection and support, in addition to cultivating profound compassion within ourselves.

Section 4:

Vision of the Lotus Sangha

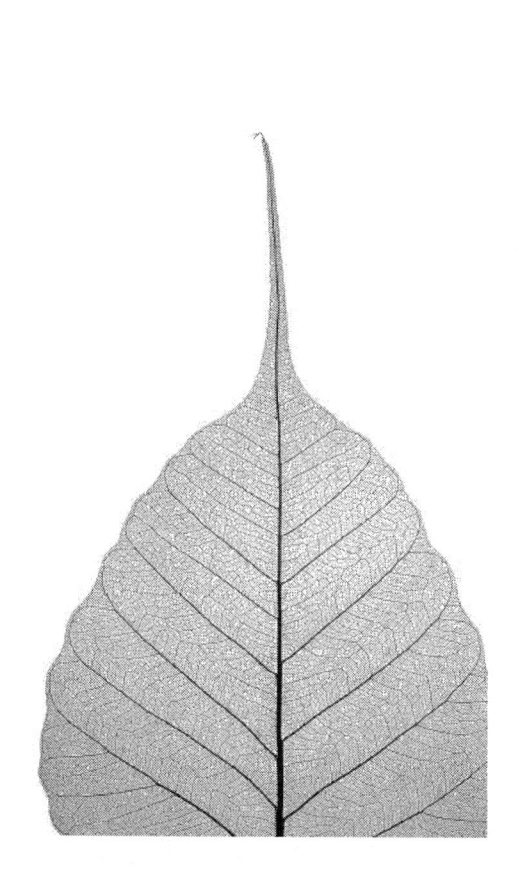

Buddhism in the Millennium

Buddhism is a global religion with great internal diversity. With more than 2,500 years of development, Buddhism has evolved by leaps and bounds with respect to philosophical doctrines, lineages, and traditions to meet the diverse needs of individuals in tandem with the zeitgeist of time. Buddhism in the 21st century is pragmatic and rational and geared to help modern people lead a value-creative life.

With the dawn of the millennium, many so-called "new age" Buddhist organizations have mushroomed and flourished in the last 50 years. These "new age" Buddhist Sangha have gradually moved away from rites and rituals to focus more on the practical aspects of Buddhist philosophies relevant to modern people. Some examples include Fo Guang Shan, Soka Gakkai, Tzu Chi, Plum Village of Thich Nhat Hanh, to name just a few.

One of the notable aspects of these Buddhist organizations is the emphasis on "Engaged" or "Humanistic" Buddhism as the way of practicing the Dharma. While conventional rituals and chanting are still relevant, more people gravitate toward pragmatic and rational teachings of Buddhism to seek solutions in dealing with a litany of challenges such as work, family, health, and relationship in daily lives.

Nichiren Buddhism is one of the most influential Buddhist sects in the 21st century, judging from the numerous Nichiren sub-sects such as Nichiren Shu, Nichiren Shoshu, Soka Gakkai, Rissho Kosei-kai, and so on. On the other hand, Western Buddhism is in the nascent stage of development. Focusing on scientific and rational understanding of Buddhism, mindfulness meditation becomes the primary practice; Western people have found a life-affirming philosophy in the Buddha's teachings of spiritual emancipation, empowerment, and enlightenment.

The Three E's of Enlightenment

With the Three One-Heart Methods as the bedrock of individual practice of the Lotus Sutra, I have conceptualized an equation of Three E's of Enlightenment, a combination of Education, Empowerment, and Engagement for the establishment of modern Sangha.

Under the aspect of Engagement, the Three M's, Methods of Music, Meditation, and Movement, are crucial to engage internally with our hearts and minds, and externally with others to practice the Dharma as a community.

> **Three E's of Enlightenment =**
>
> **Education + Empowerment + Engagement**

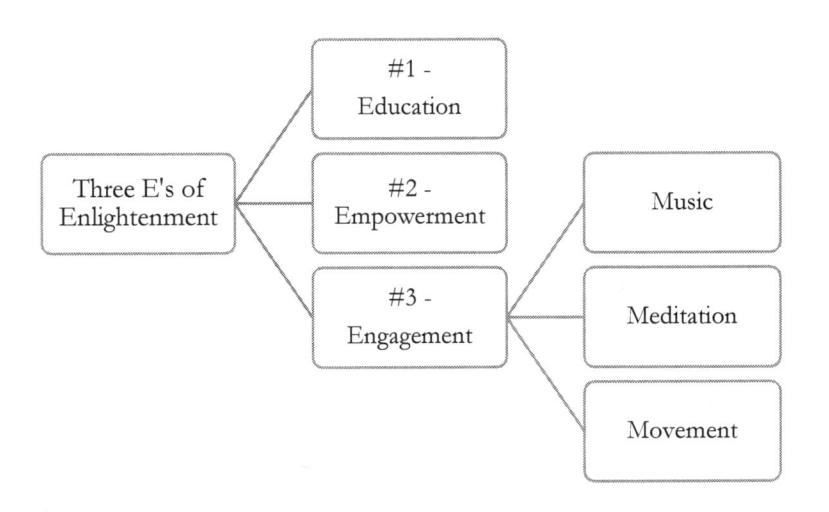

Figure 12: The Three E's of Enlightenment

1. Education

Scriptural-Based Learning of Buddhism

Education is the key to appreciating the magnificent world of Dharma. Many Buddhists around the world have limited understanding of the Buddha's teachings. For East Asian Buddhism, offering incense in the temples once in a blue moon is considered the "core" Buddhist practice. As for Western Buddhists, the boundary between secular mindfulness and Buddhism is blurred.

The optimum way to access the Dharma is to read the primary sources: the suttas or sutras. The sutra is the most direct way from which we learn the ultimate jewel of the Dharma from the Buddha himself.

Nowadays, many Buddhists learn Buddhism through secondary sources such as reading Dharma books written by Buddhist teachers. These Dharma books are mostly "personal development" types of pragmatic and application-focused Buddhist teachings. While these books certainly have their value in helping one deal with suffering and become happy, it is more empowering and satisfying to discover the Dharma from the Buddha's perspective through the sutras.

While the real authority of Dharma originates from the sutras, most Buddhist traditions focus on the Dharma teachers as the ultimate guides. In Tibetan Buddhism, the devotion to a guru is indispensable, as it is the central practice itself. Yet the scandals of Tibetan teachers such as Sogyal Rinpoche[1] calls into question the importance of having a Dharma teacher to practice Buddhism. If a person relies too excessively upon a Dharma teacher, there will come a time when he or she will become disillusioned with the Buddhist practice.

In Soka Gakkai International (SGI), the concept of "Mentor and Disciple" is one of the core practices of practicing Buddhism within the organizational context. Members of SGI ascribe all their good fortune and transformations not to the power of the Buddhist scriptures such as the Lotus Sutra but to the guidance of President Daisaku Ikeda. Some SGI members left the organization, becoming disenchanted with the perceived prevalence of a "personality cult" in SGI.[2]

Buddhist Sutras as Your Ultimate Dharma Teachers

While many Dharma teachers are worthy of respect, and while having a teacher may be pivotal for a beginner, for advanced Buddhist practitioners, the most reliable Dharma teachers are the Buddhist scriptures themselves, in addition to our own Inner Teachers within us. We need to be aware that all Dharma teachers interpret the Dharma differently according to their natures, desires, and intellectual capacities.

Moreover, external social, economic, or political conditions also influence how one deciphers the Dharma. One good example is Nichiren. His Buddhist worldviews are heavily influenced by the Japanese culture of Shintoism in the way he interpreted Buddhism, as seen in his inordinate focus on Shinto and heavenly deities in the protection of Buddhist practitioners.

In the Mahayana Mahaparinirvana Sutra, the Buddha taught his disciples to "follow the teachings, not men; the meaning, not the word; true wisdom, not shallow understanding."[3] Personally, I believe that ultimate teachers can only be found both within Buddhist scriptures as well as our own Inner Teachers. Buddhist sutras, as the primary sources, are the most reliable teachers because one can learn the true teachings directly from the Buddha himself.

The importance of learning the Dharma is reflected in the Four Bodhisattva Vows in Zen Buddhism and the Three Mahayana Refuges documented in Avatamsaka Sutra:

Four Bodhisattva Vows

> *Sentient beings are numberless; I vow to save them all.*
> *Afflictions are inexhaustible; I vow to end them all.*
> *The Dharma gates are infinite; I vow to learn them all.*
> *The Buddha-Way is unexcelled; I vow to accomplish it.*[4]

Three Mahayana Refuges

> *I take refuge in the Buddha.*
> *May all sentient beings*
> *propagate the Bodhi seeds*
> *and aspire for Buddhahood.*

> *I take refuge in the Dharma.*
> *May all sentient beings*
> *enter deeply into the treasury of the sutras*
> *and realize wisdom as deep as the ocean.*

I take refuge in the Sangha.
May all sentient beings
be capable of leading the great community
without any obstacles.[5]

An example of learning the Dharma without a teacher can be inferred from the story of Bodhisattva Never Disrespectful. What is significant about him is that he received the Dharma of the Lotus Sutra, not in an assembly setting in which a Buddha teaches in front of all disciples, but from the Buddha's voices in the sky. I suppose he might, or might not, have even known who the Buddha was (it was King of Majestic Voices Buddha) when he received the teachings in the sky. Upon hindsight, it is his immense virtues accumulated from practicing and perfecting the virtue of endurance and patience that enables him to hear the teaching of the Lotus Sutra.

Putting this in the context of learning Buddhism in the modern day, it is akin to someone who learns the Lotus Sutra, not by attending any Dharma talk delivered by a Buddhist master, but through reading the book of the Lotus Sutra itself. This does not mean that no teacher is involved; it means that a teacher in a human form is not required for one to receive the ultimate Dharma. By learning through the sutra, we receive the Dharma directly—and transcendently—from the Buddha himself, without even seeing the *real* Buddha with our mortal eyes. Therefore, be conscious in educating yourself with the Dharma through learning the Buddhist sutras, especially the Lotus Sutra. Let the Buddhist scriptures be your ultimate Dharma teachers.

2. Empowerment

Focus on Your Strengths to Unleash the Greatest Potential

Empowerment means unleashing our greatest potential by focusing on developing our strengths to the fullest. By being true to ourselves and living authentically, we will be able to maximize our natural gifts and talents to create the greatest values for humanity.

Everything in life has a true nature. Zen Buddhism teaches us to "illuminate our hearts to see our true nature. （明心见性）" There is a difference between "doing" and "being." "Doing" means deliberately attempting to "change" something that is "not you." "Being" means recognizing your innate magnificence by perceiving your true nature and living authentically. By living your true nature, you are experiencing the Four Virtues of Buddhahood—True Self, Eternity, Purity, and Happiness. Validating your true nature is honouring your own unique life path. Let us look at some examples in the Lotus Sutra:

- Maitreya was not exactly passionate about learning the Dharma. He loved fame and fortune. Yet, he becomes a Buddha.

- Maha-Kashyapa was not aspirational and intelligent, and thus he chose to practice asceticism. Yet, he becomes a Buddha.

- Devadatta was ambitious, scheming, and power-hungry. Yet, he becomes a Buddha.

Managing our shortcomings is important to prevent our Achilles' heels becoming our weakest links that derail us. However, as the saying goes, "A leopard never changes its spots." While there are certainly some benefits in improving one's weaknesses through "Human Revolution,"[6] we can never change our true nature—our fundamental personality blueprint and our DNA that makes us who we are.

Our natural gifts and talents are akin to the state of Buddhahood. The essence of the Lotus Sutra is to focus upon the Buddhahood within us. The point of empowerment is always anchored upon our strengths, talents, and natural gifts. If you wish to lead an empowering life, look within yourself to identify your True Self. By doing so, you can find your Truth North to lead you to your most creative, rewarding, and dignifying life.

Cultivate Your Inner Teacher

Apart from the Buddhist scriptures as mentioned earlier, the Inner Teacher is our Best Teacher. All people we encounter, our friends or foes, can be our teachers in some ways. Much as the external teachers are respect-worthy and beneficial, ultimately, we have to learn to listen to our inner wisdom and trust the voice of our inner Buddha in our Dharma practices. Remember, wisdom imparted by all people we encounter in life is our teacher. Having an "emotional attachment" to a particular Dharma teacher—or rather absolute devotion to a master, guru, or mentor—in order to *feel* that we have grown spiritually is not a prerequisite in the Dharma practice.

Having said that, we need to have developed a reasonably solid level of wisdom, maturity, and experience to trust our inner voice and "gut feel" as guidance. If not, one may be guided to do silly things such as committing suicide just because "voices in his head" tells him to do so.

Relying excessively on external teachers may not be practical for advanced practitioners. Self-reliance and self-empowerment is the True North if we wish to go far in life. No teacher of wisdom wants his disciples to "stick" to him like glue forever. There will come a time for the teacher to just let go of his disciples so that his disciples are free to fly high and reach the stars.

As the saying goes, "be a lamp unto yourself" and "be a refuge unto yourself."[7] Within our deepest being is an immense reservoir of potential waiting to be awakened. That's why we need to have reasonable faith and confidence in ourselves to be a trailblazer, a navigator, and an architect to walk our own life paths.

Both morality and meditation are excellent practices to cultivate our minds and spirituality. By keeping to the moral precepts as well as engaging in moments of deep silence help us to develop profound wisdom and polish our Inner Teacher.

In a nutshell, empowerment means focusing upon our strengths to touch and unveil the fullest of our possibilities. It also means cultivating our Inner Teacher and trusting our inner wisdom to do the right thing and live authentically. Be true to ourselves, we are empowered to create the optimum values for humanity.

> *"Therefore, Ananda, be islands unto yourselves, refuges unto yourselves, seeking no external refuge; with the Dhamma as your island, the Dhamma as your refuge, seeking no other refuge." – Mahaparinibbana Sutta [8]*

3. Engagement

The Three M Methods: Music, Meditation, Movement

Engagement has two aspects: first, engage our inner self through the Dharma practice; second, engage with people around us through daily interaction and sharing of the Dharma.

For the purpose of engaging our inner and outer experiences, we can apply the Three M Method: namely Music, Meditation, and Movement in the practice of the Lotus Sutra.

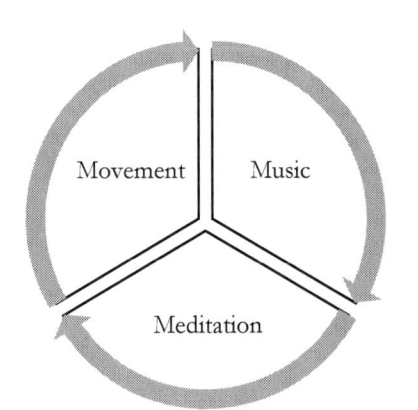

Figure 13: Three M Methods for Engagement

1. *Music as an Offering*

Dalai Lama says that happiness is the purpose of life.[9] We want to be happy practicing Buddhism so that we can experience the Joy of the Law.

Music is a celebration of happiness because it has the therapeutic power to deliver joy to the withered soul. Research has shown that music has the power to heal.[10] People of different cultures around the world celebrate momentous occasions through dance and music.

The practice of Buddhism involves giving offerings to the Buddha, Dharma, and Sangha. The act of giving will result in the accumulation of merits, virtues, and good fortune, elements of which are essential in accomplishing Buddhahood. Giving is a way to express our respect and gratitude to the Buddha and Dharma. It enables us to foster the spirit of generosity and magnanimity, as well as purify our lives.

In most Buddhist traditions and cultures, flowers, incense, fruit, lamp, oil, monetary donation, books, robes, and so on are the most common types of offerings. Melodious music, as opposed to monotonous chanting, is the type of offering that is sorely lacking.

Many Buddhist organizations in the Asian countries, such as Guang Shan, Tzu Chi, and Soka Gakkai, are actively promoting Buddhism through the culture of music. However, music remains a "side dish" or an "appetizer" in the practice of Buddhism. Thus, it is hoped that giving music as the main offering will become reality in the near future. We can trace music as a form of offering in the Lotus Sutra:

> *"If they should request others to perform music,*
> *by beating drum, blowing horn or conch shell,*
> *or playing end-blown flute, bamboo flute, zither, or harp,*
> *lute, cymbal, or gong;*
> *all these wonderful types of music*
> *are sincerely given as offerings for worship." (LS 2: 5.49)*
> *"If there are people with joyful hearts*

who sing songs to praise the Buddha's virtues,
even if they sing softly,
they have already attained Buddhahood." (LS 2: 5.50)

The Buddha replied to Bodhisattva Splendid Virtue: 'In the
remote past, there was a Buddha called King of Thunderous
Sound in the Clouds—Tathagata, Arhat, Samyak-
sambuddha. His land was called Manifestation of All Worlds
and his kalpa was called Sight of Joy. For twelve thousand
years, Bodhisattva Wonderful Music performed hundreds of
thousands of types of music and presented eighty-four thousand
seven-treasure alms bowls as offerings to King of Thunderous
Sound in the Clouds Buddha. As a result of these causes and
conditions, he has now been born in the land of Wise King of
Pure and Gorgeous Constellation Buddha, endowed with these
divine powers.' (LS 24: 2.2-2.3)

I am tremendously inspired by music as an offering to the Buddha in Chapter 24: Bodhisattva Wonderful Music. This bodhisattva is unique because he is a passionate musician who produces music as offerings to the Buddha. He cultivates his merits and virtues toward Buddhahood by doing what he does best, making music and songs. Thus, Bodhisattva Wonderful Music is an exemplary model on how to attain Buddhahood through giving music as an offering.

2. Meditation to Develop the Mind

Meditation is a wonderful practice to develop our minds and wisdom, cultivate a gentle heart of compassion, and cement our aspiration and vow to attain Buddhahood. In Buddhism, meditation practices—be they silent, seated meditation or vocal chanting—constitute the basis of Buddhist practice to develop the mind.

Generally, there are two types of silent meditation: mindfulness and samadhi. Mindfulness is a practice of paying attention at the present moment to develop insight and awareness. Samadhi is the practice of cultivating one-pointed concentration by focusing upon a single object.

In the Theravada tradition, Satipatthana or insight meditation is the core practice. As for the Mahayana tradition, samadhi meditation is the way. For example, Zen Buddhists practice seated silent meditation, and Nichiren/Pure Land Buddhists practice dynamic chanting to achieve single-point of concentration. As for Vajrayana tradition, yidam or deity meditation takes precedence.

Quotes about meditation can be found in *Appendix 3: Quotes of Meditation in the Lotus Sutra*. Here are three quotes related to meditation as excerpted from the Lotus Sutra:

> *"Those who seek the place of the Bhagavat,*
> *confident that they can become Buddhas,*
> *willing to practice meditation diligently—*
> *they belong to the category of superior medicinal herb."*
> *(LS 5: 2.28)*

> *"Again, if there are those who practice meditation*
> *and attain divine powers,*
> *having heard the Law of Emptiness,*
> *they experience exuberant joy in their hearts*
> *and emit innumerable rays of lights*
> *so as to save numerous living beings,*
> *they are the Large Tree*
> *that will grow and develop in their own ways." (LS 5: 2.38)*

> *"These living beings will have great divine powers. For instance, their bodies will glow resplendently and they will be able to fly at will. Firm in aspiration and determination, they will also be diligent and wise. Golden hue and Thirty-Two Features will adorn their bodies. All living beings in this land will only*

consume two kinds of food: first, Joy of the Law and second, Delight of Meditation." (LS 8: 1.11)

3. Movement to Propagate the Lotus Sutra

In Chapter 22: Entrustment, the Buddha entrusted his disciples to widely propagate the Lotus Sutra to benefit all people. Every disciple of the Buddha has the mission to preserve and transmit the Buddha's teachings. Thus, it is critical that we make it our personal responsibility to carry on the mission of propagating Buddhism, especially the Lotus Sutra.

> *He then touched the crowns of the bodhisattvas-mahasattvas three times before continuing with the declaration: "For immeasurable hundreds of thousands of millions of billions of asamkhya kalpas, I have practiced this Law of Supreme Perfect Enlightenment that is rare and difficult to attain. Now I have entrusted the Law to you. You must accept, embrace, read, recite, and proclaim the Law broadly so that all living beings have the opportunity to hear and understand the Law. Why? This is by virtue of the great compassion and mercy of Tathagata. He is not parsimonious, neither is he fearful. Hence, he is able to bestow upon all living beings the Buddha-wisdom, the Tathagata-Wisdom, and the Intuitive Wisdom. In essence, Tathagata is the great benefactor for all living beings. (LS 22: 1.2)*

To propagate the Dharma effectively, we need to first educate ourselves with knowledge through studying the scriptures of the Dharma. We also need to empower ourselves by polishing our morality, to unleash our greatest potentials by developing our strengths.

Achieving World Peace seems like a mirage and an elusive goal when many countries are still plagued by violence, poverty, discrimination, and human rights violations. World peace begins with us. If we cultivate our inner peace and mindful compassion through engaging with the local communities, we can become "change catalysts" to advance peaceful and harmonious co-existence in our respective countries. Here are some ideas to kick-start a Buddhist movement for the purpose of World Peace:

- Engage in cultural performances for peace
- Work with charitable organizations to help the underprivileged
- Be involved in humanitarian efforts to help those in times of natural disaster
- Participate in activities in the preservation and protection of the environment through recycling or coastal cleaning, etc.
- Participate in inter-faith dialogues to promote peaceful co-existence

No "True Buddhism" but One Buddhism

Most Nichiren sects claim that only Nichiren Buddhism, by virtue of its practice of the Lotus Sutra, is the "True Buddhism."[11] This terminology seems to imply that all non-Nichiren Buddhist schools are "untrue," which is definitely not the case. In fact, the use of the word "True Buddhism"[12] is a reflection of personal pride at best and arrogance at worst—and this is certainly inconsistent with the spirit of wisdom, inclusiveness, and compassion as taught in the Lotus Sutra.

The fact that the Lotus Sutra is declared by the Buddha as the "king of all sutras" (LS 23: 2.8) and "the first and foremost" (LS 10: 1.20) among all the Buddha's teachings does not make any of the Buddha's "provisional" teachings "untrue." Rather than refuting the early Buddha's teachings as provisional, and hence irrelevant and worthy to be brushed aside, we need to bridge the wisdom of Theravada and Mahayana Buddhism by discovering the interconnected relationships between them. A PhD Buddhist scholar once told me that if one looks deep into the suttas and sutras, they are essentially identical in terms of the Buddha's teaching of attaining Buddhahood; the only difference is the terminology or the choice of words used.

In Chapter 3, the Buddha used the metaphor of the three carriages to convey his teaching that ultimately all of us will receive the jewel of Buddhahood regardless of which Buddhist lineages, sects, or traditions we practice. Whether you choose Theravada Buddhism (Shravaka-Vehicle as symbolized by the goat carriage), Non-Buddhist teaching (Pratyekabuddha-Vehicle as symbolized by the deer carriage), or Mahayana/Vajrayana Buddhism (Bodhisattva-Vehicle as symbolized by the ox carriage), you will eventually arrive at the shore of Buddhahood by receiving the jewel of One Buddha-Vehicle of the Lotus Sutra as represented by the great white ox carriage.

Thus, the Lotus Sutra is a celebration of unity in the diversity of the Sangha, for it teaches inclusiveness by recognizing multiple pathways toward achieving Supreme Perfect Enlightenment. As such, there is no "True Buddhism," but rather One Buddhism that unites all seemingly contradictory Buddhist philosophies into One Dharma of Buddhahood. By recognizing the inclusive teaching of the Lotus Sutra, we will realize that it is downright pointless to assert superiority of one's sect over another through righteous refutation in the name of justice.

Conclusion

To establish a Sangha from the ground up in the new millennium, the Three E's of Enlightenment—Education, Empowerment, and Engagement—is the recommended method.

First, we need to understand and appreciate the Dharma through scriptural-based learning of the sutras. The Buddhist scriptures are our ultimate Dharma teachers. By devoting ourselves to education of the Dharma through the sutras, we will strengthen our faith and joy in the Dharma practice.

133

Second, we need to be empowered through developing our strengths to the fullest and cultivating our Inner Teacher. It is through self-leadership can we have the confidence to spread the Dharma and live a fulfilling life.

Third, we need to engage our internal self through the Dharma practice, and external self through interacting with others. The Three M Methods of Music, Meditation, and Movement are ways to engage ourselves and others creatively and pragmatically for the purpose of advancing World Peace through the Dharma.

Section 5:

Mandala of the Lotus Sutra

Object of Devotion

One of the most intriguing aspects of Nichiren Buddhism is the object of devotion or Buddhist mandala known as the Gohonzon. Different Nichiren sects have different versions of the Gohonzon with slightly different contents. The various Gohonzons inscribed by Nichiren or his successive priests are often mirrors of their worldviews with respect to their interpretation of the Lotus Sutra.

For example, the Gohonzon of Nichiren Shu[1], which is known to be the closest replica of Nichiren, has a few more beings which are absent in the Nichikan Gohonzon of the Soka Gakkai. Some of these beings include Bodhisattva Manjushri, Bodhisattva Universal Worthy, Bodhisattva Maitreya, Bodhisattva Medicine King, Shariputra, Mahakashyapa, Ajatashatru, Devadatta, Master Miaol-lo, etc.

The many different versions of Gohonzon can, ironically, become a bone of contention among diverse Nichiren sects. Some Nichiren sects assert the legitimacy of their Gohonzon by claiming the existence of some "superpower" in the Gohonzon while denigrating other versions of Gohonzon as "slandering the Law."[2]

About Nichiren Gohonzon

The contents of the Gohonzon are often the reflections of the personal belief and worldview, interpretation and philosophical stance of the Buddhist priest who inscribes it. While there is no "right or wrong" in terms of the style of object of worship, factors such as personal preference and the comfort level of having certain beings included in the object of worship do play a part in choosing a mandala.

Nichiren's philosophy and worldview are influenced by the Japanese Shinto beliefs and the doctrines of Zhiyi, especially Ichinen Sanzen, which results in the inclusion of all types of beings in the Gohonzon. Much as Nichiren was devoted to the Lotus Sutra, he was not spared from Shinto belief with respect to the protection of heavenly gods. This is clearly seen in the *Gosho*:

- The protection granted by heavenly gods[3] and Shinto deities[4]

- The incorporation Shinto deities such as Sun Goddess and Hachiman (Sun of War) in the Gohonzon

Apart from that, Nichiren also included in the Gohonzon various deities such as the Indian Vedic gods of Sun, Moon, and Star, the wrathful Vajrayana deities of Acalanatha Vidyaraja and Ragaraja Vidyaraja.[5] All these are the testaments to his belief in the protection of gods and deities more than the protection by Buddhas and bodhisattvas as documented in the Lotus Sutra:

"…Hundreds of thousands of Buddhas will protect and guard you with their divine powers." (Ls 23: 2.16).[6]

"…You should know that after Tathagata has entered parinirvana, if there are those who copy, embrace, read, or recite this sutra, give offerings, and expound it for others, Tathagata will shield them with his robe and Buddhas living in other regions will protect and keep them in mind." (LS 10: 2.3)[7]

"O Infinite Intention! Bodhisattva Avalokitesvara possesses such mighty divine powers that bring benefits to many people. Hence, living beings should always be mindful of him."
(LS 25: 1.10)[8]

At that moment, Bodhisattva Medicine King said to the Buddha: 'O Bhagavat! I wish to give the dharani to the Teachers of the Law so as to guard and protect them.' (Lotus Sutra 26: 1.4) [9]

In Nichiren Gohonzon, Buddhas and bodhisattvas constitute only about 20% of all the beings. The other 80% of the beings include Shinto gods such as Hachiman (God of War) and Sun Goddess, wrathful Dharma protectors popular in Shingon Buddhism such as Wisdom King Immovable (Skt Achala) and Wisdom King Craving-Filled (Skt Ragaraja), to mention just a few.

One of the controversial beings is the presence of Devil King of the Sixth Heaven (King Mara). Although King Mara is mentioned in the Lotus Sutra, he did not join the assembly to listen to the Lotus Sutra. Moreover, he is not entirely considered to be the ally or Dharma protector of the Buddha's teachings. Some people may argue that the King Mara represents the "fundamental darkness" in our lives, just as the state of Hell is part of the Ten Worlds (principle of the mutual possession of the Ten Worlds), it remains doubtful if it is appropriate to include King Mara in the Gohonzon.

In view of the above, it helps to be mindful that Nichiren's inclusion of the various deities is a testament to his personal belief as well as the cultural influence of Japan on his interpretation of Buddhism. By having Nichiren Gohonzon as the object of devotion, one is unwittingly embracing an eclectic mix of "Buddhism" that incorporates elements of Shintoism, Hinduism, and esoteric/tantric Buddhism.

Mandala of the Lotus Sutra

I always believe that the mandala of the Lotus Sutra should focus purely upon the realm of Buddhahood. This means that only Buddhas and bodhisattvas are included in the mandala. Non-Buddhahood-related beings, be they good or bad, should not be included at all. The reason is simple: what we pay attention to every day in our daily ritual becomes who we are. A mandala is a sacred object that works like a mirror. If we focus upon Buddhahood, we become a Buddha. If we focus upon all kinds of beings in the Ten Worlds, we will unconsciously be distracted and adulterated, which, in turn, will become a stumbling block in our journey to attaining Buddhahood. Thus, it is critical that we focus on the Law of Buddhahood as our core Dharma practice.

Prayer, chanting, and meditation are sacred rituals to cultivate our minds. By constantly being mindful of Buddhahood within the depths of our lives, we will achieve single-pointed concentration (samadhi) to awaken, polish, and illuminate our inner worlds of Buddhahood.

Three Major Differentiations

With the awareness of the pros and cons of Nichiren Gohonzon, I have created an innovative mandala that reflects my conviction that the mandala of the Lotus Sutra should focus only upon the state of Buddhahood. The following are three major differentiations between Nichiren Gohonzon and the mandala of the Lotus Sutra:

1. Only Buddhas and Bodhisattvas found in the Lotus Sutra

Influenced by Zhiyi's philosophy of Ichinen Sanzen (mutual possession of the Ten Worlds) as well as the Japanese culture of Shintoism, Nichiren included a full spectrum of beings in the Gohonzon.

In contrast, the mandala of the Lotus Sutra focuses only on the state of Buddhahood and the direct teachings of the Lotus Sutra, as opposed to the "derived" doctrines created by a Buddhist master. Therefore, only the most important Buddhas and bodhisattvas who can be traced back to the Lotus Sutra are selected and included in the mandala of the Lotus Sutra for the benefit of Buddhist practitioners.

2. No Shinto, Hindu, or wrathful gods and deities

While many of the heavenly gods or wrathful deities are benevolent beings who are known to protect the Dharma and the practitioners of the Lotus Sutra, the Buddha has not given instructions for his disciple to worship them. As such, all types of non-Buddhahood beings such as local Japanese deities, Hindu gods, wrathful Dharma protectors or beings are excluded.

In fact, Shakyamuni Buddha had expressly instructed his disciples to pay homage to Bodhisattva Avalokitesvara, but this bodhisattva that personifies compassion is prominently absent in the Gohonzon.

3. Focus on the Dharma, not the Person

Focusing on the Dharma, rather than any person, is the most reliable way of practicing Buddhism. In Mahayana Mahaparinirvana Sutra, the Buddha taught his disciples to "follow the teachings, not men; the meaning, not the word; true wisdom, not shallow understanding."[10]

Hence, consistent with the Buddha's teachings of focusing on the Dharma instead of any person, the names of all Buddha's disciples and Buddhist masters, such as Nichiren, high priests of Nikko-lineages, Zhiyi, Miao-lo, Dengyo, Shariputra, and Mahakashyapa, are excluded.

10 Inspirations behind the Design of the Mandala

There are two words to sum up the essence of the Lotus Sutra: Wisdom and Compassion. The Buddha's wisdom is Supreme Perfect Enlightenment, and the essence of the Buddha's life and spirit is

141

Compassion. Buddhas and bodhisattvas are the ultimate embodiments of unsurpassed wisdom and infinite compassion.

Keeping the three major differentiations in mind, I have created the mandala with deep joy and gratitude to the Law of Buddhahood. I am convinced that this mandala will one day be a source of immeasurable blessings and good fortune to benefit humanity in the odyssey of attaining Buddhahood.

I am delighted with share with you the reasoning behind my innovative creation of the mandala of the Lotus Sutra in ten inspirational points:

Figure 14: Mandala of the Lotus Sutra

Inspiration #1: Lotus Flower

The first impression of the mandala of the Lotus Sutra is the lotus flower. This lotus represents the essence of the Lotus Sutra, the Law of White Lotus, or the Law of Buddhahood. There is no better way to represent the wisdom of Lotus Sutra metaphorically other than the image of the lotus flower because the lotus is the ultimate symbol of the wonderful Dharma of Anuttara Samyak Sambodhi.

Similar to Nichiren Gohonzon, five large Chinese characters of the Lotus Sutra—Miao Fa Lian Huang Jing (妙法蓮华经)—are written vertically in the middle of the lotus. The presence of the large title of the Lotus Sutra in Chinese characters helps the practitioners to focus on the wisdom of Supreme Perfect Enlightenment as taught in the Lotus Sutra.

Inspiration #2: Eight Petals

In Chapter 7, Shakyamuni Buddha revealed his past rebirth as the youngest of the sixteen sons of Great Astuteness and Surpassing Wisdom Buddha.[11] Shakyamuni Buddha and his fifteen brothers had already attained Buddhahood in the remote past.

The eight petals of the lotus flower wonderfully depict the sixteen princes who were already Buddhas in the eight directions. These fifteen Buddhas share an intimate connection with Shakyamuni Buddha because they are his brothers. The presence of these Buddhas is significant for a number of reasons. First, they are concrete examples of Shakyamuni Buddha's attainment of Buddhahood eons ago. This is consistent with his revelation of eternal lifespan and his attainment of Buddhahood in the remote past in Chapter 16. Second, it reveals that Shakyamuni Buddha is not the only Buddha because Buddhas are everywhere in the Universe:

> *"O monks! Now I shall reveal to you that these sixteen shramanas, the disciples of the Buddha, have already attained Supreme Perfect Enlightenment. Everywhere in the ten*

directions, they are currently expounding the Law, with immeasurable hundreds of thousands of millions of billions of bodhisattvas and shravakas as their followers.

"In the eastern region, there are two Buddhas: one is known as Akshobhya who lives in the Land of Joy while the other is named Sumeru Peak.

"As for the southeastern region, there are two Buddhas: one is named Lion Voice while the other is named Lion Appearance.

"In the southern region, there are two Buddhas: one is named Space Dwelling and the other is named Eternal Extinction.

"In the southwestern region, there are two Buddhas: one is named Emperor Appearance while the other is named Brahma Appearance.

"In the western region, there are two Buddhas: one is named Amida, the other is named Saving All from the Suffering of the World.

"In the northwestern region, there are two Buddhas: one is named Tamalapatra Sandalwood Fragrance Divine Power and the other is named Sumeru Appearance.

"In the northern region, there are two Buddhas: one is named Cloud Freedom, the other is named King of Cloud Freedom.

In the northeastern region, there are two Buddhas: one is named Destroyer of All Worldly Fear and the sixteenth is I, Shakyamuni Buddha, who attained Supreme Perfect Enlightenment in this Saha land." (LS 7: 4.13)

Inspiration #3: The Treasure Pagoda with Two Buddhas

> *"Meanwhile, Abundant Treasures Buddha offered half his seat in the Treasure Pagoda to Shakyamuni Buddha, saying: 'O Shakyamuni Buddha! Take a seat over here!' At once, Shakyamuni Buddha entered the pagoda and seated himself in cross-legged position on half the seat." (LS 11: 2.24)*

Similar to Nichiren Gohonzon, two Buddhas—Shakyamuni Buddha and Abundant Treasures Buddha—are present on both sides of the Chinese character of the Lotus Sutra, Miao Fa Lian Hua Jing (妙法莲华经).

This depiction is an inspiration from Chapter 11 in which a seven-jewelled treasure pagoda emerged from the earth and suspended in mid-air. Inside the pagoda was the Abundant Treasures Tathagata who had long ago entered parinirvana, and Shakyamuni Buddha who was invited by Abundant Treasures Tathagata to join him. The five Chinese characters of the Lotus Sutra represent the Treasure Pagoda.

Inspiration #4: Bodhisattva Manjushri

> *'O Maitreya! You should know that Bodhisattva Splendid Light who lived at that time was none other than I myself while Bodhisattva Seeker of Fame was you. Now when I witness this auspicious sign, it is no different from what I had seen before. I surmise that today Tathagata is going to expound the Great Vehicle sutra known as The Lotus Sutra—the Law to guide bodhisattvas, the Law protected and mindfully guarded by Buddhas.' (LS 1: 3.14)*

Bodhisattva Manjushri is considered the oldest and most significant bodhisattva associated with prajna, or transcendental wisdom, in Mahayana Buddhism. Found in Mahayana sutras such as the

145

Prajnaparamita Sutra and the Avatamsaka Sutra, he is the yidam, or meditational deity, in Tibetan Buddhism. In Chinese Buddhism, he is one of the Four Great Bodhisattvas; the three other bodhisattvas are Kṣitigarbha, Avalokitesvara, and Samantabhadra. He and Bodhisattva Samantabhadra also form the Trinity of Shakyamuni Buddha.

In Chapter 1 of the Lotus Sutra, Bodhisattva Manjushri revealed his past identity as Bodhisattva Splendid Light who was the teacher of Bodhisattva Maitreya in the remote past. In Chapter 12, Bodhisattva Manjushri was a teacher who guided the dragon daughter to attain Buddhahood solely by teaching her the Lotus Sutra. In Chapter 14, Bodhisattva Manjushri expounded the ways to practice the Lotus Sutra with peace and joy.

Inspiration #5: Bodhisattva Universal Worthy

> *Thereafter, Shakyamuni Buddha extolled him, saying:*
> *"Excellent, excellent! O Universal Worthy! Because you are*
> *able to shield and support the Lotus Sutra for the peace, joy,*
> *and benefit of all living beings, you have already accomplished*
> *extraordinary merits and displayed profound compassion. Since*
> *the remote past, you have already awakened a desire to attain*
> *Supreme Perfect Enlightenment and have taken a vow to use*
> *your divine powers to guard and protect the Lotus Sutra. I will*
> *use my divine powers to guard and shield those who are able to*
> *accept and embrace the name of Bodhisattva Universal*
> *Worthy." (LS 28: 2.1)*

Bodhisattva Universal Worthy (Skt. Samantabadra) is an eminent bodhisattva in the Mahayana tradition. In Chinese Buddhism, he forms the Trinity of Shakyamuni Buddha and also one of the Four Great Bodhisattvas. In the Nyingma school of Tibetan Buddhism, he is regarded as the Adi-Buddha (i.e. First Buddha or Primordial Buddha) who is presented in indivisible Yab-Yum (Buddhist symbol) with his consort Samantabhadri as a way to depict the primordial union of wisdom and compassion.

In Avatamsaka Sutra, he guided Sudhana to follow Bodhisattva Avalokitesvara in the practice of achieving enlightenment. Moreover, he is well-known to have made ten vows to achieve Buddhahood:[12]

1. To pay homage and respect to all Buddhas
2. To praise the Tathagata
3. To offer abundant offerings generously
4. To repent misdeeds and evil karmas
5. To rejoice in others' merits and virtues
6. To request the Buddhas to continue teaching
7. To request the Buddhas to remain in the world
8. To follow the teachings of the Buddhas at all times
9. To accommodate and benefit all living beings
10. To transfer all merits and virtues to benefit all beings

In Chapter 28 of the Lotus Sutra, Bodhisattva Universal Worthy joined the congregation just before Shakyamuni Buddha wrapped up his teaching. He came to offer encouragement, support, and protection to the practitioners of the Lotus Sutra. He also gave assurance to Shakyamuni Buddha with respect to widespread propagation of the Lotus Sutra in the Saha world.

The closing sutra of the Lotus Sutra—The Sutra of Meditation on Bodhisattva Universal Worthy—is essentially a teaching of meditation upon emptiness as a way of purifying all past negative karma for the purpose of attaining Buddhahood quickly.

Inspiration #6: Bodhisattva Maitreya

> *"He will be the next Buddha*
> *with the name Maitreya,*
> *who will broadly save all living beings*
> *in numbers beyond measure." (LS 1: 4.36)*

In Cakkavatti Sutta[13] of the Pali Canon, Bodhisattva Maitreya was predicted by Shakyamuni Buddha to be the next future Buddha. In Chapter 1 of the Lotus Sutra, Bodhisattva Manjushri declared that Bodhisattva Maitreya will be the next Buddha to succeed Shakyamuni Buddha.

Bodhisattva Maitreya appeared many times in the Lotus Sutra as the leader who asked Shakyamuni Buddha questions in Chapters 1, 15, 16, and 18. In Chapter 16, he beseeched Shakyamuni Buddha three times to preach the Dharma.

Inspiration #7: Bodhisattva Medicine King

> *The Buddha spoke to Bodhisattva Flower King of Constellation: "Who do you think Bodhisattva Joyfully Seen by All Living Beings was? He was none other than the present Bodhisattva Medicine King! His offerings of self-sacrifice amount to immeasurable hundreds of thousands of millions of billions of nayuta of numbers. (LS 23: 2.1)*

Bodhisattva Medicine King is an important figure as he appeared in the Lotus Sutra numerous times: chapter 1, 10, 13, 23, and 26. In Chapter 23: History of Bodhisattva Medicine King, the Buddha narrated the past life story of Bodhisattva Medicine King who practiced the Dharma by giving abundant of offerings to Pure and Brilliant as the Sun and Moon Buddha.

His practice is similar to the past life ascetic practices of Shakyamuni Buddha in that he did not hesitate to sacrifice his limbs and life for the sake of Dharma.

Inspiration #8: Bodhisattva Wonderful Music

> *"O Splendid Virtue! Bodhisattva Wonderful Music is able to save and protect various living beings in the Saha world. Bodhisattva Wonderful Music transforms and manifests himself in different forms so as to expound the Lotus Sutra for*

all living beings in the Saha world. Yet his divine powers, his transformations, and his wisdom will never deteriorate."
(LS 24: 2.8)

Bodhisattva Wonderful Music practiced the Dharma by giving music as an offering to King of Thunderous Sound in the Clouds Buddha. This bodhisattva saved people in the Saha world through his divine powers by skillfully transforming into various physical forms to lead people to enlightenment.

This bodhisattva is special because he does not dwell in the Saha world, and his name is not mentioned is any of the Mahayana sutras except the Lotus Sutra.

Inspiration #9: Bodhisattva Avalokitesvara

"O Infinite Intention! This Bodhisattva Avalokitesvara has accomplished merits by transforming into various forms and traveling throughout the lands to save living beings. Hence, all of you should wholeheartedly give offerings to Bodhisattva Avalokitesvara." (LS 25: 1.17)

Bodhisattva Avalokitesvara is the bodhisattva of profound benevolence and compassion. There are innumerable temples dedicated to Bodhisattva Avalokitesvara in China, Korea, and Japan— a testament to the immense popularity of Bodhisattva Avalokitesvara is among Mahayana Buddhists. In Tibetan Buddhism, the Dalai Lama is considered as the reincarnation of Bodhisattva Avalokitesvara. Thus, it is bewildering and perplexing that the famous name of Bodhisattva Avalokitesvara is virtually non-existent in Tendai and Nichiren Buddhism.

Bodhisattva Avalokitesvara appears in many Mahayana sutras such as the Nilakantha Dharani Sutra, the Karandaavyuha Sutra, and the Heart Sutra. In Chapter 25 of the Lotus Sutra, the Buddha urged his disciples to give offerings to Bodhisattva Avalokitesvara wholeheartedly and always be mindful of his name for divine protection in times of adversity.

Inspiration #10: Four Bodhisattvas of the Earth

> *Meanwhile, through the divine powers of the Buddha, the four groups saw the bodhisattvas filling the empty space of immeasurable hundreds of thousands of millions of billions of lands. Among these bodhisattvas were the four leaders. The first leader was called Superior Actions, the second leader was called Boundless Actions, the third leader was called Pure Actions, and the fourth leader was called Steadfast Actions. These four bodhisattvas were the foremost teachers and leaders among the assembly. (LS 15: 1.8)*

Nichiren considered himself to be the reincarnation of Bodhisattva Superior Actions.[14] The Nikko-lineage of Nichiren Buddhism, Soka Gakkai and Nichiren Shoshu, regards Nichiren as the "Original Buddha" (Adi-Buddha) and rejects the contentions of other Nichiren sects that view him as a bodhisattva.[15]

The primary reason why the four bodhisattvas of the earth are included is the emergence of the four leaders of the bodhisattvas of the earth—Superior Actions, Boundless Actions, Pure Actions, and Steadfast Actions—in response to the summons of Shakyamuni Buddha in Chapter 15. To benefit living beings in the Saha world, the Buddha entrusted the propagation of the Lotus Sutra in the Saha world to the four leaders of the bodhisattvas of the earth instead of the bodhisattvas from the other lands.

Number Reference to the Mandala of the Lotus Sutra

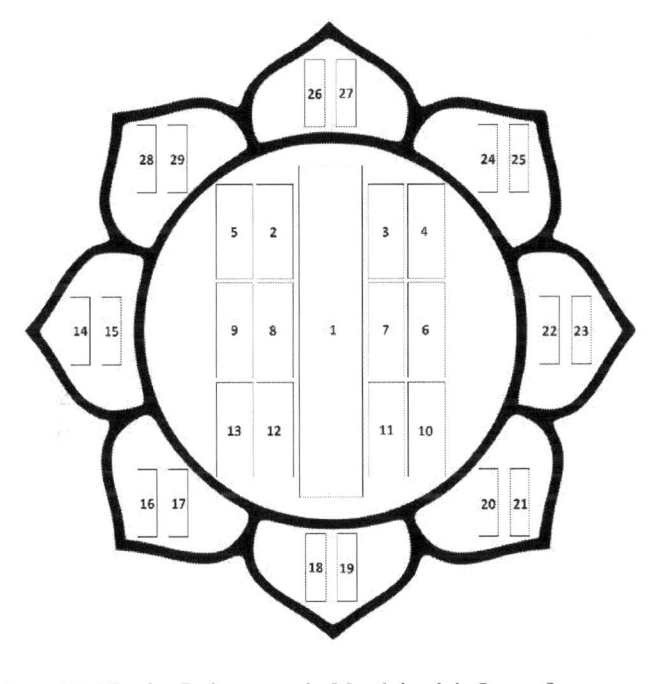

Figure 15: Number Reference to the Mandala of the Lotus Sutra

No.	Name in English	Name in Chinese
1	Lotus Sutra of the Magnificent Law	妙法莲华经 (Miao Fa Lian Hua Jing)
2	Shakyamuni Buddha	释迦年尼佛 (Shi Jia Mou Ni Fo)
3	Abundant Treasures Tathagata	多宝如来 (Duo Bao Ru Lai)
4	Bodhisattva Manjushri	文殊师利菩萨 (Wen Shu Shi Li Pu Sa)
5	Bodhisattva Universal Worthy	普贤菩萨 (Pu Xian Pu Sa)

151

6	Bodhisattva Avalokitesvara	观世音菩萨 (Guan Shi Yin Pu Sa)
7	Bodhisattva Wonderful Music	妙音菩萨 (Miao Yin Pu Sa)
8	Bodhisattva Medicine King	药王菩萨 (Yao Wang Pu Sa)
9	Bodhisattva Maitreya	弥勒菩萨 (Mi Le Pu Sa)
10	Bodhisattva Superior Actions	上行菩萨 (Shang Xing Pu Sa)
11	Bodhisattva Boundless Actions	无边行菩萨 (Wu Bian Xing Pu Sa)
12	Bodhisattva Pure Actions	净行菩萨 (Jing Xing Pu Sa)
13	Bodhisattva Steadfast Actions	安立行菩萨 (An Li Xing Pu Sa)
14	Akshobhya Buddha	阿閦佛 (A Chu Fo)
15	Sumeru Peak Buddha	须弥顶佛 (Xu Mi Ding Fo)
16	Lion Voice Buddha	师子音佛 (Shi Zi Yin Fo)
17	Lion Appearance Buddha	师子相佛 (Shi Zi Xiang Fo)
18	Space Dwelling Buddha	虚空住佛 (Xu Kong Zhu Fo)
19	Eternal Extinction Buddha	常灭佛 (Chang Mie Fo)
20	Emperor Appearance Buddha	帝相佛 (Di Xiang Fo)
21	Brahma Appearance Buddha	梵相佛 (Fan Xiang Fo)
22	Amida Buddha	阿弥陀佛 (A Mi Tuo Fo)

23	Saving All from the Suffering of the World Buddha	度一切世间苦恼佛 (Du Yi Qie Shi Jian Ku Nao Fo)
24	Sumeru Appearance	须弥相佛 (Xu Mi Xiang Fo)
25	Tamalapatra Sandalwood Fragrance Divine Power	多摩罗跋栴檀香神通佛(Duo Mo Luo Ba Zhan Tan Xiang Shen Fo)
26	Cloud Freedom	云自在佛(Yun Zi Zai Fo)
27	King of Cloud Freedom	云自在王佛(Yun Zi Zai Wang Fo)
28	Destroyer of All Worldly Fear Buddha	坏一切世间怖畏佛 (Huai Yi Qie Shi Jian Bu Wei Fo)
29	Shakyamuni Buddha	释迦牟尼佛 (Shi Jia Mou Ni Fo)

Conclusion

The Mandala of the Lotus Sutra[16] is a beautiful object of devotion that captures the essence of the Lotus Sutra by focusing only upon the state of Buddhahood.

Free of the eclectic cultural influences of Shintoism, Hinduism and esoteric Buddhism, this mandala does not include any gods or deities. Moreover, consistent with the Buddha's teachings of relying on the Dharma rather than any persons, this mandala also excludes the names of Buddha's disciples and the Dharma teachers. Instead, only the Dharma of Buddhahood expressed in the five Chinese characters of the Lotus Sutra, as well as the most important Buddhas and bodhisattvas who can be traced back to the Lotus Sutra, are included in the mandala.

Summary and Final Thoughts

Buddhism is the ultimate teaching of emancipation, empowerment, and enlightenment through attaining Buddhahood. While there are countless pathways to reach the pinnacle of Buddhahood, the Lotus Sutra is a wonderful Dharma that teaches us the special and direct method of attaining Buddhahood quickly through a scripture that is infused with the immense wisdom, profound compassion, and divine powers of the Eternal Buddha. What makes the Lotus Sutra unique is not merely the Buddha-wisdom, but the Buddha's immeasurable benevolence, grace, and compassion to transcendently support his disciples to accomplish Buddhahood.

Triple Refuge and the Three Gifts

The Three Gifts offered by the Buddha are: the Gift of the Law (Dharma), the Gift of Life (Buddha), and the Gift of Love (Sangha). The Triple Gems are interwoven in the fabric of the Lotus Sutra. By embracing the Lotus Sutra, we are literally taking the Triple Refuge.

The Gift of the Law is the Buddha's teaching of the One Buddha-Vehicle, which means the Dharma of Anuttara Samyaka Sambodhi, for the universal enlightenment of all living beings. The One Buddha-Vehicle is akin to the Bodhi seed which has to be planted in the fertile soil of our Buddha-nature (potentiality) in order for the tree of enlightenment to sprout and bloom in our lives.

The Gifts of Life have two aspects: first, revelation of the Dharmakaya of an Eternal Buddha (wisdom); second, the Buddha's secret life-to-life transmission of merits and virtues to support his disciples in attaining Buddhahood quickly (compassion). As the Lotus Sutra is a sacred scripture infused with the divine powers of the Buddha, one can attain Buddhahood through a scriptural-based approach of practice.

The Gift of Love means the divine salvation through the divine powers by Bodhisattva Avalokitesvara. As for application in daily life, compassion can be manifested through such virtues as patience, generosity, charity, and filial piety to the people around us.

As such, the Three Gifts is considered to be a "Special Method" because the gifts are the Buddha's grace, unconditional love, and profound compassion bestowed to his disciples to enable them to achieve Supreme Perfect Enlightenment quickly.

Buddha in the Sky: Emptiness, Middle Way, Buddhahood

The Buddha in the Sky, a metaphoric image appearing in the Ceremony of the Air in the Lotus Sutra, is the teaching of the Three Ultimate Truths of Emptiness, Middle Way, and Buddhahood. Unlike Zhiyi's Threefold Truths of Emptiness, Middle Way, and Falseness, the Three Ultimate Truths includes the Truth of Buddhahood. The Three Ultimate Truths is a philosophical breakthrough because it delineates the interconnected relationships between Emptiness, Middle Way, and Buddhahood previously unexplained by Nagarjuna and Zhiyi.

The Law of Emptiness is a creative Law present in an unconditional world. It contains the truth of Infinity, Purity (which is connected to happiness), and Eternity (which is connected to True Self).

The Law of Middle Way is the truth as it appears in a conditioned world. It contains the truth of the Skillful Means and the truth of the Law of Cause and Effect (i.e. Dependent Origination and Twelve-linked Chains of Causation). Thus, the Law of Emptiness is not identical with the Law of Middle Way as previously propounded by both Nagarjuna and Zhiyi. In other words, the Law of Emptiness and the Law of Middle Way are mutually exclusive.

The Law of Buddhahood is the oneness of the Law of Emptiness and the Law of Middle Way. While the Law of Emptiness and the Law of Middle Way are mutually exclusive, the Law of Buddhahood is the transformational agent that integrates the Law of Emptiness and the Law of Middle Way. Nevertheless, the warp and woof of the Law of Buddhahood is that of the Law of Emptiness. It is only under specific conditions that the Law of Buddhahood is manifested as the Law of Middle Way.

The significance of the Law of Buddhahood is that we are already endowed with the Buddha-nature to attain Buddhahood. Irrespective of whether we practice the Law of Emptiness (Bodhisattva-Vehicle), Law of Middle Way (Shravaka-Vehicle) or the Law of Buddhahood (Buddha-Vehicle), we are certain to achieve Supreme Perfect Enlightenment.

Three One-Heart Methods

The Three One-Heart Methods is the comprehensive practice of the Lotus Sutra. Method #1 is to practice the Lotus Sutra with faith through the nine ways: accept, embrace, read, recite, understand, explain, copy, write, and have right mindfulness.

Method #2 is to propagate the Lotus Sutra to benefit all living beings. Method #3 is to practice mindfulness of Bodhisattva Avalokitesvara to cultivate great compassion. The Three One-Heart Methods is a Middle-Way approach of holistic practice because it encompasses the principles of both the Self-Power (Jiriki) and Other-Power (Tariki) to attain Buddhahood.

Vision of the Lotus Sangha

The Three E's Equation of Enlightenment—Education, Empowerment, and Engagement—is the framework to establish the Sangha of the new millennium in the practice of the Lotus Sutra. Through scriptural-based learning of the Lotus Sutra (Education), focusing on unleashing our greatest potential to the fullest (Empowerment), and engaging internally with our minds and externally through interactions with people (Engagement), we can enable the Lotus Sangha to develop resplendently in the millennium.

Mandala of the Lotus Sutra

The Mandala of the Lotus Sutra is a splendid object of devotion to enable all Buddha's disciples to awaken, cultivate, and consolidate the Law of Buddhahood within their hearts and minds. A non-Nichiren object of worship that is free from the cultural influence of Shintoism, the mandala excludes Hindu gods and Shinto deities and focuses instead on the Buddhas and bodhisattvas who can help practitioners awaken and polish their Buddhahood within.

Final Thoughts

What makes Buddhism stands out from the rest is that it teaches the wisdom of the true nature of life as well as the methods to be liberated from the suffering of the process of birth, aging, illness, and death.

Without the Buddha's teachings of Buddhahood, there is no way one is able to gain release from the inexorable bondage governed by the Law of Karma (i.e. Law of Cause and Effect). Thus, the greatest spiritual miracle is none other than the extinction of rebirth through becoming a Buddha.

In essence, Buddhism is a teaching of unsurpassed enlightenment that results in personal empowerment and spiritual emancipation. Consistent with the title of this book, *Mindfulness of Buddhahood in Life,* the key to practice begins with mindfulness upon the lofty state of Buddhahood within the depths of our lives. With the Lotus Sutra—the Dharma of Anuttara Samyak Sambodhi—as the cornerstone of the practice, all of us will surely arrive at the Eagle Peak of Supreme Perfect Enlightenment.

Epilogue

The greatest blessing in my life was to have encountered the Lotus Sutra at a very young age. Life would have been meaningless had it not been for the Buddha's teachings and the Lotus Sutra. I am deeply grateful to have the golden opportunity to practice the Lotus Sutra through chanting the daimoku, Nam Myoho Renge Kyo.

The incredible power of chanting the daimoku is irrefutable. This simple practice truly gives me immeasurable good fortune to fulfill most of my dreams and aspirations in life. Thus, I am eternally grateful to Nichiren for introducing such a simple and yet effective method of practicing the Lotus Sutra through chanting the daimoku.

Chanting enables us to awaken and polish our Buddha-nature within to create value in life. Whenever I was down in the spiritual quagmire or experienced a maelstrom of turbulent emotions, chanting soothed my embattled heart by bringing me much peace and calm. When life threw a curve to me, shattering my dreams, it was chanting that gave me a flickering hope to stand up again and bounce back. In the darkest times of my life, every daimoku is the prayer of hope. It is this hope that enables me to pull myself up by my own bootstraps.

I experience a gamut of emotions ranging from bliss, gratitude, repentance, determination, faith, and peace during my chanting sessions. Most of the time, I chant like a river, flowing peacefully. Sometimes, I chant like a horse galloping vigorously in the meadow. Experiences of chanting like a lion king are few and far between.

Nevertheless, there was one time when I chanted so powerfully, like a lion king with a stentorian voice, that I somehow entered into the Buddha's realm. I could literally feel the true essence of Buddha-Tathagata gushing out within me, expanding like a golden light shining forth from the deepest depth of my being. The experience was truly and indescribably phenomenal. At that moment, I knew that my pure true self is the Buddha. This rare experience is proof that all sentient beings are already endowed with the Buddha potential within them. All it takes is to awaken the giant within us.

Apart from chanting, I practice silent meditation regularly. Some Nichiren practitioners think that vocal chanting and silent meditation are identical, but I beg to differ. As someone who is aspirational and self-driven, I am prone to anxiety and worries due to the constant sense of urgency in completing tasks according to schedules. Silent meditation with deep breathing gives me tremendous sense of inner peace and relaxation. I feel settled and grounded after a short 10 minutes of meditation. Thus, I am convinced that a balance of dynamic vocal chanting and silent seated meditation is the key to the ultimate Dharma practices.

Dreams are messages from the divine. When I did the translation of the Lotus Sutra in 2014, I had several dreams related to the Buddha. Once, I dreamed of my past life as a Theravada Dharma teacher performing initiation and empowerment to a line of disciples.

I also dreamed of myself reaching the top of a snow-capped mountain and saw President Ikeda surrounded by his followers. A few days after this, I dreamed of myself praying to a smiling Guan Yin in a temple. A week later or so, I saw a golden Buddha and I found myself pedalling upstream against the current in a river teeming with many gigantic pink lotuses. Along the years, I once saw two golden Buddhas in my dream—a four-armed Chenrezig and Shakyamuni Buddha.

I always believe that for advanced practitioners of Buddhism, the Buddhist sutras are the ultimate teachers. Apart from relying upon the scriptures as the bedrock of Buddhism, we also need to have faith in our Inner Teacher as the spiritual guidance. By listening to our inner wisdom and trusting in our inner Buddha's voices, we are empowered to focus on our talents and unleash our greatest potential to create tremendous values for the peace, happiness, and prosperity of humanity.

I am convinced that we need to practice Buddhism with a sense of deep joy and gratitude in our hearts. It is the positive emotions anchoring to the Joy of Dharma that brings us to perceive "One Buddhism"—as opposed to "True Buddhism"—that unites the internal diversity within the Sangha. My greatest wish in life is to witness a beautiful flourishing in the diversity of Sangha so that people with different dispositions and aspirations can savour the Joy of Dharma through practicing the Lotus Sutra in a joyful, innovative, and empowering manner.

Love is not what we say; love is what we do. Let us connect our hearts as One Buddha to experience the bliss scaling the pinnacle of Supreme Perfect Enlightenment together! May you always be happy, healthy, and wise!

Appendices

Appendix 1: 10 Quotes of Buddhahood in the Lotus Sutra[1]
Quote #1:

> *"Since all of you are awakened to the fact that*
> *all Buddhas, the Teachers of the Worlds,*
> *apply the expedient methods to teach the Law,*
> *have no further doubts and*
> *let your hearts be filled with immense joy!*
> *For you know you will also become Buddhas!" (LS 2: 5.100)*

Quote #2:

> *"Now, for you and the rest*
> *I preach the truth—*
> *none of you is shravaka*
> *seeking to attain parinirvana.*
> *All of you are actually pursuing*
> *the way of a bodhisattva.*
> *So long as you gradually learn and practice,*
> *in no time you will all become Buddhas." (LS 5: 2.41)*

Quote #3:

> *The Buddha said to Medicine King: "Furthermore, after*
> *Tathagata has entered parinirvana, if there is one person who*
> *hears even one stanza or one phrase of the Lotus Sutra and*
> *experiences a momentary joy, I shall also bestow on this person*

the prophecy of attaining Supreme Perfect Enlightenment."
(LS 10: 1.2)

Quote #4:

Thereupon, knowing that the bodhisattvas had requested three times consecutively, the Bhagavat proclaimed: "O disciples! Listen carefully to the secret divine powers of Tathagata! All heavenly gods, humans, and asuras in the entire Universe believe that the present Shakyamuni Buddha, who left the palace of Shakya not far from the city of Gaya, attained Supreme Perfect Enlightenment at the sanctuary of the Way. O virtuous men! In truth, however, it has been immeasurably boundless hundreds of thousands of millions of billions of nayuta kalpas since I became a Buddha." (LS 16: 1.3)

Quote #5:

"Having acquired merits upon hearing with joy the eternal lifespan of the Buddha, these virtuous men and women will definitely attain Supreme Perfect Enlightenment." (LS 17: 2.3)

Quote #6:

"O Gainer of Great Authority! Who do you think this Bodhisattva Never Disrespectful was at that time? This person is none other than I myself! In my previous lifetime, had I not accepted, embraced, read, recited, and expounded the Lotus Sutra for others, I would never have been able to attain Supreme Perfect Enlightenment so quickly. Because I accepted, embraced, read, recited, and expounded the Lotus Sutra for others in the presence of the former Buddhas, I was able to quickly attain Supreme Perfect Enlightenment."
(LS 20: 1.15)

Quote #7:

> *"After my parinirvana,*
> *a person of wisdom should embrace the Lotus Sutra*
> *upon hearing the merits and benefits.*
> *People such as these*
> *will definitely be able*
> *to attain Buddhahood." (LS 21: 2.14)*

Quote #8:

> *At that time, Shakyamuni Buddha rose from his Dharma seat*
> *and then displayed his great divine powers by using his right*
> *hand to touch the crowns of immeasurable bodhisattvas-*
> *mahasattvas. After which, he proceeded to make the*
> *declaration: "For immeasurable hundreds of thousands of*
> *millions of billions of asamkhya kalpas, I have practiced this*
> *Law of Supreme Perfect Enlightenment that is rare and*
> *difficult to attain. Now, I have entrusted the Law to you. You*
> *must wholeheartedly focus on widely propagating the Law so as*
> *to bring increased benefits, blessings, and prosperity for all."*
> *(LS 22: 1.1)*

Quote #9:

> *At that moment, Bodhisattva Upholder of the Earth rose from*
> *his seat immediately and said in front of the Buddha: "O*
> *Bhagavat! If there are living beings who hear this chapter of*
> *Bodhisattva Avalokitesvara—his effortless deeds, his*
> *universal manifestation of divine powers as the universal*
> *gateway to the Lotus Sutra—one should know that the merits*
> *and blessings accumulated by these people will be abundant!"*
> *When the Buddha expounded this chapter of Universal*
> *Gateway, eighty-four thousand people in the assembly conceived*
> *the aspiration of attaining Supreme Perfect Enlightenment.*
> *(LS 25: 2.25)*

Quote #10:

> *"O Universal Worthy! During the last five hundred years after the parinirvana of Tathagata, anyone who sees those who accept, embrace, read, and recite the Lotus Sutra should think as such: "Before long, these people will arrive at the sanctuaries of enlightenment, vanquish the armies of devils, and attain Supreme Perfect Enlightenment. They will turn the Wheel of the Law, beat the drum of the Law, blow the conch of the Law, shower the rain of the Law, and sit on the lion thrones of the Law amidst the great assembly of heavenly gods and humans."* (LS 28: 2.4)

Appendix 2: 10 Quotes of Emptiness in the Threefold Lotus Sutra[2]

Part 1: Lotus Sutra

Quote #1:

"However, Tathagata understands the Law of one form and one flavor—namely the form of deliverance, the form of dissociation, and the form of dissolution—as well as the ultimate nirvana of eternal tranquillity that will eventually return to its original emptiness. The Buddha fully comprehends these but he does not immediately expound the perfect wisdom to all living beings because he wishes to protect them after having perceived the desires in their minds." (LS 5: 1.11)

Quote #2:

"Again, if there are those who practice meditation
and attain divine powers,
having heard the Law of Emptiness,
they experience exuberant joy in their hearts
and emit innumerable rays of lights
so as to save numerous living beings,
they are the Large Tree
that will grow and develop in their own ways." (LS 5: 2.38)

Quote #3:

"Throughout the long night,
we practiced the Law of Emptiness,
so as to be liberated from the Threefold World
and the bitter pains of trials and tribulations.
Dwelling in the final existence,
we expected to attain the partial nirvana." (LS 4: 2.45)

Quote #4:

> "*O monks! If Tathagata knows of his impending parinirvana and knows that the people in the assembly are pure, firm in faith and understanding, have perceived the Law of Emptiness, and are able to enter deep meditation, then he will gather the assembly of bodhisattvas and shravakas to expound the Lotus Sutra for them. In this Universe, there are no two Vehicles to attain parinirvana; for true extinction can only be achieved via the one and only Buddha-Vehicle.*" (LS 7: 4.17)

Quote #5:

> "*Furthermore, he had a perfect understanding of the Law of Emptiness expounded by the Buddhas. Having acquired the Four Unhindered Wisdoms, he was able to expound with clarity. Free of doubt and confusion, he had fully developed the divine powers of bodhisattvas. Lifetime after lifetime, he consistently carried out pure Brahma practices. Therefore, he was recognized as a true shravaka for all people living in the era of that particular Buddha.*" (LS 8: 1.5)

Quote #6:

> "*The sanctuary represents*
> *a mind of great mercy and compassion;*
> *the robe represents*
> *a heart of gentleness and patience;*
> *the throne represents*
> *the awareness of emptiness in all phenomena.*
> *These are the three principles to apply*
> *when the Lotus Sutra is expounded.*" (LS 10: 2.19)

Quote #7:

Even before he had finished his reply, innumerable bodhisattvas seated on the jeweled lotus flowers emerged from the oceans and arrived at Eagle Peak, where they remained elevated in the air. These bodhisattvas had all been taught, transformed, and saved by Manjushri. Those who had mastered bodhisattva practice were having a discussion on the Six Paramitas. Those shravakas who previously carried out the shravaka's practices in midair were now practicing the Mahayana's Principle of Emptiness. Manjushri said to Accumulated Wisdom: "These are the people in the oceans who were taught by me." (LS 12: 3.5)

Quote #8:

"Next, bodhisattvas-mahasattvas should view all phenomena as being intrinsically empty in order to correctly perceive their true nature, which has no topsy-turvy, no movement, no regression, and no evolvement. It is like an empty nothingness without intrinsic nature and beyond the expression of word. There is no birth, no emerging, no arising, no name, no form, no substantial existence, no quantity, no boundary, no hindrance, and no obstruction. All phenomena arise by reason of causation; and they are commonly explained in an inverted manner by reason of creation." (LS 14:1.8)

Quote #9:

"Why is this so? Because Tathagata completely perceives the true characteristics of the Threefold World as they are: there is no birth or death, no ebbing or arising. Neither is there present existence and subsequent extinction, substantial reality or fictitious imagination, same or different. These characteristics of realities are not what one perceives them to be while living in the Threefold World. Tathagata has clearly and unmistakably seen all these." (LS 16: 1.11)

Quote #10:

> *"Again, if someone—irrespective of whether he is guilty or not—being shackled by manacles, fetters, cangues, or chains should call upon the name Bodhisattva Avalokitesvara, then his shackles will be destroyed, setting him free." (LS 25: 1.7)*

Part 2: Immeasurable Meanings Sutra

> *The Buddha replied: "O virtuous men! This single doctrine is known as the Immeasurable Meanings. If any bodhisattvas wish to practice and learn the Immeasurable Meanings, then they should observe and perceive that all realities are originally—from the beginning and continue to be—empty and tranquil in nature and aspect; there is neither large nor small, neither birth nor death, neither abiding nor moving, neither advancing nor retreating, just an empty space with no dualism. (IMS 2:1.6)*

Part 3: The Sutra of Meditation on Bodhisattva Universal Worthy (MBUW)

Quote #1 – Meditation upon Emptiness is the Method of Repentance

> *"The true aspect of reality is that of birthlessness and deathlessness. What is sin? What is blessing? My mind is effortlessly empty; sin and blessing have no master. The truth of all realities is neither abiding nor decaying. Therefore, you should repent in this manner: meditate upon the mind that has no real mind, understand that reality does not comply with the Law, and perceive that all realities are the truth of emancipation, of nirvana, of tranquility. This method of contemplation is called the Great Repentance, Adorned Repentance, and Sinless Repentance as well as the Annihilation of the Conscious Mind. By practicing repentance*

in this way, you will achieve purification of your body and mind.
Without dwelling in the Law, you will experience freedom like
the flowing water. As you continue to constantly focus on these
thoughts, you will meet Bodhisattva Universal Worthy and the
Buddhas in the ten directions." (MBUW 7.5)

Quote #2 – The Teaching of Law of Emptiness is for the Bodhisattva

"Thereupon, the Bhagavats will expound the Law of No
Aspect for you through the brilliant light of great compassion.
You as the practitioner will therefore hear the teaching of the
Foremost Principle of Emptiness. Having heard the teaching
without fear, you will immediately attain the status of
bodhisattva." (MBUW 7.6)

Quote #3 – Meditate upon the Law of Emptiness to Expiate all Unwholesome Karma

"After the parinirvana of the Buddha, if there are any of the
Buddha's disciples who adhere to the Buddha-words by
practicing this repentance, you should know that these people
are carrying out the actions of Universal Worthy. Those who
carry out the practices of Universal Worthy will not encounter
any malicious manifestations or experience any evil
retributions. If there are living beings who make obeisance to
the Buddhas in the ten directions six times every day and night,
recite the Great Vehicle sutra, and ponder upon the profound
Law of Emptiness of the foremost in meaning and principle,
then it only takes the time of a snap of a finger for them to
eliminate the sins of birth and death accumulated over hundreds
of millions of billions of asamkhya kalpas." (MBUW 9.4)

Quote #4 – Read and Study the Mahayana Sutras

The Buddha spoke to Ananda: "I, along with the bodhisattvas
in the Wise Kalpa and the Buddhas in the ten directions, am

able to wipe out the sins of birth and death accumulated over hundreds of millions of billions of asamkhya kalpas as a result of pondering the true meaning of the Great Vehicle. As a consequence of practicing the supremely wonderful method of repentance, each of us has been able to become Buddhas in the ten directions. If you wish to quickly attain Supreme Perfect Enlightenment or if you wish to meet Bodhisattva Universal Worthy and the Buddhas in the ten directions in your present lifetime, then you should read, recite, and ponder the meaning of the Great Vehicle in a secluded place. This should be done after you have taken a shower to purify yourself, donned clean attire, and burnt outstanding incense." (MBUW 9.2)

Quote #5 – Connect the Minds with the Wisdom of Emptiness to Achieve Purification of Life

"O people of wisdom! Therefore, if there are shravakas who fail to observe the three precepts, five precepts, eight precepts, the precepts of a monk, the precepts of a nun, the precepts of a novice monk, the precepts of a novice nun, the precepts of a shikshamana, or various rules of dignified conduct out of ignorance, ill-will, or malice, if they wish to eradicate these sins and return to the ways of a monk who observes the rules of shramana, then they should diligently read and practice this equal and impartial sutra, ponder the profound Law of Emptiness—the foremost in meaning—in order to connect their minds with the wisdom of emptiness. You should know that these people will completely eliminate all their sins and transgressions forever through every instant of their meditative thoughts. This practice is called Mastering the Rules of Shramana and Perfection in the Mastery of Dignified Conduct. These people are worthy of receiving offerings from all heavenly gods and humans." (MBUW 9.11)

Quote #6 – First Method of Repentance: Meditation of the Law of Emptiness

The Buddha said: "What are the methods of repentance for Kshatriyas and ordinary citizens? People who carry out the methods of repentance should maintain an honest mind, refrain from slandering the Three Treasures, and refrain from causing harm or making it difficult for those who carry out Brahma practices. Rather, they should focus their minds on practicing the six methods of thought and making offerings to support those who embrace the Great Vehicle. Instead of performing any acts of worship, they should meditate upon the profound Law of Emptiness of the foremost in meaning. People who practice these methods are carrying out the First Method of Repentance for Kshatriyas and Ordinary Citizens." (MBUW 9.14)

Quote #7 – Second Method of Repentance: Filial Piety toward Parents, Teachers, and Elders

"People who carry out the second act of repentance should practice filial piety toward their father and mother, as well as be respectful toward their teachers and seniors. This is known as the Second Method of Repentance." (MBUW 9.15)

Quote #8 – Third Method of Repentance: Use the Correct Law to Govern a Country to Prevent the Oppression of People

"People who carry out the third act of repentance should adopt the True Law in governing the country so as to prevent the oppression of people. This is known as the Third Method of Repentance." (MBUW 9.16)

Quote #9 – Fourth Method of Repentance: Six No-Killing Days

"People who carry out the fourth act of repentance should, within their powers of sovereignty or authority, decree six days of purification in which no acts of killing are allowed. This

practice is known as the Fourth Method of Repentance."
(MBUW 9.17)

Quote #10 – Fifth Method of Repentance: Deep Faith in the Law of Cause and Effect, the Dharma of Buddhahood, and the Truth of the Eternal Buddha

"People who carry out the fifth act of repentance should have deep faith in the Law of Cause and Effect, believe in the Way of One Single Truth, and understand that the Buddha is eternal without ever entering parinirvana. This is known as the Fifth Method of Repentance." (MBUW 9.18)

Appendix 3: 20 Quotes of Meditation in the Lotus Sutra[3]

Quote #1

"If there are living beings
who have encountered many former Buddhas,
upon hearing the Law, they practice
generosity, morality, forbearance,
diligence, meditation, and wisdom,
thus cultivating an abundance of blessings and insight;
these people have already
attained Buddhahood." (LS 2: 5.38)

Quote #2

"All living beings who are liberated from the Threefold World
will obtain the joy of Buddhas such as the joy of meditation, the
joy of emancipation, and other similar delightful toys. Because
of their ability to generate pure and wonderful joy of the first-
rate, they are of one single form and one single type that is
extolled by sages." (LS 3: 4.27)

Quote #3

"Those who understand the impeccable Law
are able to attain nirvana,
Six Divine Powers,
and Three Understandings,
living in solitude in the forested mountains,
always practicing meditation
to achieve the state of pratyekabuddhas—
they belong to the category of mediocre medicinal herb."
(LS 5: 2.27)

Quote #4

"Those who seek the place of the Bhagavat,
confident that they can become Buddhas,

willing to practice meditation diligently—
they belong to the category of superior medicinal herb."
(LS 5: 2.28)

Quote #5

"Again, if there are those who practice meditation
and attain divine powers,
having heard the Law of Emptiness,
they experience exuberant joy in their hearts
and emit innumerable rays of lights
so as to save numerous living beings,
they are the Large Tree
that will grow and develop in their own ways." (LS 5: 2.38)

Quote #6

"We arrive from
five hundred trillion lands.
Putting aside our joy of deep meditation,
we come all the way to worship the Buddha." (LS 7: 3.8)

Quote #7

"O monks! If Tathagata knows of his impending parinirvana
and knows that the people in the assembly are pure, firm in
faith and understanding, have perceived the Law of Emptiness,
and are able to enter deep meditation, then he will gather the
assembly of bodhisattvas and shravakas to expound the Lotus
Sutra for them. In this Universe, there are no two Vehicles to
attain parinirvana; for true extinction can only be achieved via
the one and only Buddha-Vehicle." (LS 7: 4.17)

Quote #8

"These living beings will have great divine powers. For instance,
their bodies will glow resplendently, and they will be able to fly

at will. Firm in aspiration and determination, they will also be diligent and wise. Golden hue and Thirty-Two Features will adorn their bodies. All living beings in this land will only consume two kinds of food: first, Joy of the Law and second, Delight of Meditation." (LS 8: 1.11)

Quote #9

At that instant, all the attendees in the assembly caught sight of the whole body of Abundant Treasures Tathagata engaged in meditation on a lion throne inside the Treasure Pagoda. The next moment, they heard him say: "Excellent, excellent! O Shakyamuni Buddha! I am here to listen to your teaching of the Lotus Sutra!" (LS 11: 2.22)

Quote #10

Manjushri replied: "Yes, the Dragon King Sagara's daughter, who has just turned eight years old. Wise and intelligent, she readily understands the karma of all living beings. Having obtained the dharani, she is able to embrace and uphold the profound Secret Treasury as revealed by the Buddhas. She is also able to enter deep meditation and achieve full understanding of various doctrines. In an instant, she is awakened to the aspiration of enlightenment and attains the stage of non-regression. She has acquired an unhindered eloquence and a compassionate mind that treats all living beings as her children. Her merits are accomplished. Her thoughts and discourses are as subtly wonderful as they are magnanimous. Compassionate and benevolent in disposition, gentle and elegant in determination, she has attained enlightenment."
(LS 12: 3.10)

Quote #11

"Arising from meditation,
they should expound the Lotus Sutra

179

> *eloquently and persuasively*
> *for the kings and rulers,*
> *princes, ministers, and ordinary citizens,*
> *Brahmans and the rest.*
> *Their minds should be*
> *valiantly at peace." (LS 14: 2.20)*

Quote #12

> *"Again, they will find themselves*
> *in the midst of mountains and forests,*
> *practicing the benevolent Law*
> *and receiving actual proof of the Truth of Reality.*
> *Deep in meditation,*
> *they will meet Buddhas in the ten directions." (LS 14: 7.22)*

Quote #13

> *"What the Buddha has expounded is exactly like this. It has not been long since the Buddha attained the Way. Nevertheless, the great multitude of bodhisattvas have been diligently advancing the Buddha-Way for immeasurable thousands of millions of billions of kalpas. They are capable of entering into immeasurable hundreds of thousands of millions of billions of samadhi meditations, hence obtaining great divine powers." (LS 15: 3.6)*

Quote #14

> *"Competent in handling questions,*
> *they are fearless.*
> *Patient and resolute,*
> *they are righteous, majestic, and virtuous.*
> *They have been praised by the Buddhas in the ten directions*
> *for their excellent skills in differentiated explanation.*
> *Instead of taking delight among the humans,*

they enjoy engaging in meditation." (LS 15: 3.15)

Quote #15

"Dwelling alone
in secluded places for countless kalpas,
be it sitting or walking,
with the exception of sleeping,
they always control and meditate their minds." (LS 17: 2.11)

Quote #16

"Upholding the blessings of a focused mind,
they seek only to attain the unsurpassed Way, thinking:
'I will attain the perfect wisdom
through the mastery of meditation.'" (LS 17: 2.13)

Quote #17

"They will always be respectful of pagodas and temples,
maintain humble attitude toward monks,
keep a distance from people of excessive arrogance,
and practice meditation to develop wisdom." (LS 17: 3.21)

Quote #18

"Those who embrace the Lotus Sutra
are able to know by scenting,
the location of a multitude of monks
who are earnestly practicing the Law
by reading or reciting the Lotus Sutra
while sitting or walking around,
or by practicing seated meditation with focus
under trees in the forests." (LS 19: 3.31)

Quote #19

> *"The two sons were endowed with great divine powers, blessings, virtues, and wisdom as a result of practicing the bodhisattva way for a long time. They had thoroughly understood and completely mastered thirty-seven types of beneficial methods to the Way—namely the paramita of generosity, paramita of morality, paramita of perseverance, paramita of diligence, paramita of meditation, paramita of wisdom, and paramita of expedient methods as well as benevolence, compassion, joy, and non-attachment."* (LS 27: 1.3)

Quote #20

> *"Eventually, I will not use the inferior vehicles*
> *to save and liberate all living beings.*
> *The Buddha abides in the Great Vehicle,*
> *through which he attains the Law.*
> *Adorned by the strength of meditation and wisdom,*
> *he brings deliverance for all."* (LS 2: 5.18)

Appendix 4: 10 Quotes of Happiness in the Lotus Sutra[4]

Quote #1:

Happiness is…Becoming a Buddha

> *"Since all of you are awakened to the fact that*
> *all Buddhas, the Teachers of the Worlds,*
> *apply the expedient methods to teach the Law,*
> *have no further doubts and*
> *let your hearts be filled with immense joy!*
> *For you know you will also become Buddhas!" (LS 2: 5.100)*

Quote #2:

Happiness is…Experiencing Joy upon Hearing the Lotus Sutra

> *The Buddha said to Medicine King: "Furthermore, after*
> *Tathagata has entered parinirvana, if there is one person who*
> *hears even one stanza or one phrase of the Lotus Sutra and*
> *experiences a momentary joy, I shall also bestow on this person*
> *the prophecy of attaining Supreme Perfect Enlightenment."*
> *(LS 10: 1.2)*

Quote #3:

Happiness is…Receiving the Prophecy of Attaining Buddhahood with Exhilaration

> *"Today, when we hear the prediction from the Buddha directly*
> *that shravakas can attain Supreme Perfect Enlightenment, we*
> *are exhilarated at gaining an unprecedented experience! We*
> *consider ourselves deeply fortunate to hear the exceptional Law*
> *because we have received great benefits and an abundance of*
> *precious treasures without actively seeking them!" (LS 4: 1.3)*

Quote #4:

Happiness is…Joy of the Law and Delight of Meditation.

> *"These living beings will have great divine powers. For instance,*
> *their bodies will glow resplendently, and they will be able to fly*

at will. Firm in aspiration and determination, they will also be diligent and wise. Golden hue and Thirty-Two Features will adorn their bodies. All living beings in this land will only consume two kinds of food: first, Joy of the Law and second, Delight of Meditation." (LS 8: 1.11)

Quote #5:

Happiness is...Bringing Joy to the Buddha through Embracing the Lotus Sutra

"Those who are able to embrace the Lotus Sutra
are bringing immense joy
to I myself and my emanated bodies,
as well as the departed Abundant Treasures Buddha."
(LS 21: 2.8)

Quote #6:

Happiness is...Sharing the Lotus Sutra with Exuberance

"Those who embrace the Lotus Sutra
will experience inexhaustible joy
in explaining the meanings of the Law
using diverse names and linguistic expressions—
just like the breeze in the air,
moving gracefully without hindrance." (LS 21: 2.11)

Quote #7:

Happiness is...Propagating the Lotus Sutra with Great Jubilation

When the bodhisattvas-mahasattvas heard the Buddha-words, joy and jubilation suffused their bodies. With even greater reverence and respect, they prostrated, lowered their heads, and pressed their palms together before facing the Buddha and speaking sonorously in unison: "O Bhagavat! Have no worries

on this! We will definitely carry out the tasks according to the
guidance of the Bhagavat!" (LS 22: 1.5)

Quote #8:

Happiness is…Giving Offering to All Buddhas by Praising the Law

"If there are those who hear the Law and praise it delightfully,
even if it is only one word of praise,
these people have already given offerings
to Buddhas in the three existences.
They are very rare indeed,
rarer than the udambara flower." (LS 2: 5.93)

Quote #9:

Happiness is…Singing Songs of Praise to the Buddha's Virtues

"If there are people with joyful hearts
who sing songs to praise the Buddha's virtues,
even if they sing softly,
they have already attained Buddhahood." (LS 2: 5.50)

Quote #10:

Happiness is…Simply Giving Joy to People

"O virtuous men! If there are living beings who approach me,
I will use my Buddha's eyes to observe their faith and assess
their faculties. Then, depending on the capacity and degree of
receptiveness of each individual, I will adapt my approach of
salvation accordingly. I will appear in many places and
expound to them under different names or different age groups.
Sometimes, I will also speak about my entering of nirvana.
Moreover, I expound the exquisitely Magnificent Law using a
myriad of expedient methods for the joy and happiness of all
living beings." (LS 16: 1.8)

Appendix 5: *Overview Summary of the 28 Chapters of the Lotus Sutra*[5]

The Lotus Sutra is all about attaining Buddhahood. Below is chapter-by-chapter summary that focuses on the aspect of Buddhahood in the Lotus Sutra:

Chapters	Key Teachings Related to Buddhahood
Chapter 1 – Introduction	Bodhisattva Maitreya is declared by his past teacher, Bodhisattva Manjushri, as the next Buddha after Shakyamuni Buddha. *"He will be the next Buddha* *with the name Maitreya,* *who will broadly save all living beings* *in numbers beyond measure."* *(LS 1: 4.36)*
Chapter 2 – Expedient Methods	The Buddha reveals the Law of Buddhahood as the One Buddha-Vehicle, the Dharma of Supreme Perfect Enlightenment. *"O Shariputra! You should wholeheartedly accept and embrace the words of the Buddha with faith and understanding. The words of all Buddha-Tathagata are the truth: there are no alternative Vehicles, only the One Buddha-Vehicle."* *(LS 2: 4.15)*
Chapter 3 – The Parable	Two key points: 1) The Buddha bestows prophecy of Buddhahood to Shariputra.

	2) Through the Parable of the Blazing House, the Buddha illustrates the meaning of One Buddha-Vehicle: regardless of which Buddhist traditions you practice, you will eventually attain Buddhahood through the One Buddha-Vehicle in the Lotus Sutra. *"O Shariputra! In view of the causes and conditions, you should understand that all Buddhas apply the power of expedient methods to teach the One Buddha-Vehicle by differentiating them in three different ways." (LS 3: 4.29)*
Chapter 4 – Faith and Understanding	Mahakashyapa narrates the Parable of Father and His Lost Son to further illustrate the meaning of the One Buddha-Vehicle: *"As for the Buddha-wisdom, the Bhagavat has never been parsimonious as we are actually the children of the Buddha since time without beginning. However, because we were fond of the inferior teachings, the Buddha did not immediately teach us the Great Vehicle. Should we have had a loftier aspiration in seeking the Great Law, the Buddha would have long expounded the teaching of the Great Vehicle for us. Now, the*

	Buddha has finally revealed the One Vehicle in this sutra." (LS 4: 1.24)
Chapter 5 – Parable of the Medicinal Herbs	The Buddha further illustrates the One Buddha-Vehicle through the Parable of the Medicinal Herbs. This parable explains the true identity of the Buddha as the supremely transcendental being who teaches in an equitable manner. It also teaches that everyone, irrespective of nature, desire, or capacity, is capable of becoming a Buddha. *"Then, he declares to the great assembly: 'I am Tathagata, Worthy of Offerings, Perfect in True Wisdom and Enlightenment, Perfect in Knowledge and Conduct, Well-Liberated, the Omniscient, the Almighty, Master Trainer, Teacher of Heavenly Gods and Humans, Buddha-Bhagavat. For those who have not gained deliverance, I will deliver them. For those who have not been enlightened, I will enlighten them. For those who have not been peaceful, I will bestow peace for them. For those who have yet to attain nirvana, I will lead them to nirvana. I understand the present and future lifetimes just as they are. I am the Omniscient. I am the Omnispective. I know the Way, I open the Way, and I expound the Way."* (LS 5: 1.7)

Chapter 6 – Prophecies of Attaining Buddhahood	The Buddha bestows prophecy of Buddhahood to Mahakashayapa, Maudgalyayana, Subhuti, and Maha-Katyayana.
	"At that time, the Bhagavat, having proclaimed the stanzas, declared to the great assembly: The disciple of mine, Maha-Kashyapa, will be able to meet three hundred trillion Buddhas-Bhagavats in future lifetimes to whom he will give generous offerings, reverence, respect, and praises. He will also widely propagate the infinite Great Law of the Buddhas. In his final incarnation, he will become a Buddha with the name Resplendent Tathagata." (LS 6: 1.1)
Chapter 7 – Parable of the Imaginary City	The Buddha illustrates the meaning of One Buddha-Vehicle through Parable of the Imaginary City: the expedient teachings are not the ultimate teachings, they are merely for people to recharge in the long journey of Buddhahood.
	"The Buddha, knowing the weak and shallow minds of living beings, uses the power of expedient methods to teach two nirvanas so as to provide a resting place along the journey. If living beings continue to dwell in these two stages (i.e., shravakas and pratyekabuddhas), Tathagata will then give this guidance: 'Your task has not been accomplished. The stage

	where you are dwelling is close to the Buddha-wisdom. However, you must observe and perceive that the nirvana you have attained is not the real one. Tathagata applies the expedient methods to make a distinction by expounding the One Buddha-Vehicle into three.'" (LS 7: 5.7)
Chapter 8 – Prophecy of Buddhahood for the Five Hundred Disciples	Chapter Eight contains two key points: 1) The Buddha bestows prophecies of Buddhahood by Purna and Kaundinya. 2) The Buddha teaches the importance of Dharma friends in the journey of attaining Buddhahood through the Parable of the Jewel in the Robe. *"O Bhagavat! Now we understand the truth that we are in fact bodhisattvas who have been predicted to attain Supreme Perfect Enlightenment. Because of this, we are exhilarated at gaining an unprecedented experience!"* *(LS 8: 3.6)*
Chapter 9 – Prophecies for Arhats, Apprentices, and Proficient Ones	The Buddha bestows prophecy of attaining Buddhahood to Ananda and Rahula, even though both of them have yet to attain arhatship, as well as two thousand apprentices and the proficient disciples.

	"Thereafter, the Buddha said to Rahula: 'In your future lifetime, you will become a Buddha with the name Walking on Flowers of Seven Treasures Tathagata, Worthy of Offerings, Perfect in True Wisdom and Enlightenment, Perfect in Knowledge and Conduct, Well-Liberated, the Omniscient, the Almighty, Master Trainer, Teacher of Heavenly Gods and Humans, Buddha-Bhagavat. You will give offerings to Buddhas and Tathagata as numerous as the dust particles in the ten worlds. You will be also be born as the eldest son of those Buddhas, just as you are my son now.'" (LS 9: 3.1)
Chapter 10 – Teachers of the Law	The Buddha declares that all who respond with joy upon hearing the Lotus Sutra will attain Buddhahood. Moreover, the Buddha asserts that the Lotus Sutra is the cause for quick attainment of Buddhahood. *"However, if the person hears about the Lotus Sutra, ponders and practices it, then you should know that this person is very near Supreme Perfect Enlightenment. Why? Because all bodhisattvas attain Supreme Perfect Enlightenment through the Lotus Sutra. This sutra opens the*

	gateway of expedient methods and reveals the true nature of phenomena. The treasury of the Lotus Sutra is deeply hidden so that it is not within easy reach. Yet now, the Buddha teaches, transforms, and leads the bodhisattvas to attaining enlightenment by opening and revealing the truth for them." *(LS 10: 2.8)*
Chapter 11 – Sighting of the Treasure Pagoda	Chapter Eleven contains two key points: 1) The Treasure Pagoda symbolizes the Dharmakaya of the Buddha. This shows that both Abundant Treasures Buddha and Shakyamuni Buddha have already realized the Dharmakaya. 2) Through the example of Abundant Treasures Buddha, the Buddha wants to make an important point about the power of a vow. A vow for Buddhahood is most invincible; it will help one to overcome all hurtles to successfully achieve enlightenment. *"...In a robust and sonorous voice, he asked the four groups of people: 'Who is able to broadly expound the Lotus Sutra in this Saha world? Now is the perfect time to do so. Tathagata will enter nirvana soon and the Buddha wishes to entrust the Lotus Sutra to someone who can propagate it for eternity.'" (LS 11: 2.26)*

Chapter 12 – Devadatta	The Buddha expounds that both evil people and women can attain Buddhahood. Physical, exterior forms are merely illusions. *"Because Devadatta was a good friend of mine, I was able to fully master Six Paramitas; develop benevolence, compassion, joy, and non-attachment; and be endowed with Thirty-Two Features, Eighty Types of Physical Elegance, purplish-golden skin, the Ten Powers, Four Kinds of Fearlessness, Four Social Rules, Eighteen Distinctive Qualities, and Divine Powers of the Way. Hence, the reason I was able to attain Supreme Perfect Enlightenment to widely save all living beings was solely due to the good friend of mine—Devadatta."* (LS 12: 2.2)
Chapter 13 – Encouragement to Embrace the Law	The Buddha bestows prophecies of Buddhahood to nun Mahaprajapati and Yashodhara. Understanding the challenges involved in propagating the Lotus Sutra, bodhisattvas from other lands make a vow to fulfill their missions in spreading the Dharma. *"We are the emissaries of the Bhagavat!* *We have absolutely no fear of these people!* *We will expound the Law eloquently!* *May the Buddha dwell in peace and ease!"* (LS 13: 3.19)

Chapter 14 – Expounding with Peace and Joy	Apart from teaching his disciples how to practice the Law of Lotus with peace and joy, the Buddha also uses the Parable of the Precious Pearl in the Topknot to illustrate the One Buddha-Vehicle as the ultimate gift of supreme Dharma of the Buddha. *"O Manjushri! The Lotus Sutra is the Secret Treasury of all Buddhas-Tathagatas. The Lotus Sutra is the foremost among all sutras. For many long nights, I have mindfully guarded and protected the sutra; never have I expounded the sutra indiscriminately. Today, for the very first time, I have decided to proclaim the Lotus Sutra for all of you." (LS 14: 6.10)*
Chapter 15 – Emerging from the Earth	The emergence of Bodhisattvas of the Earth, including the four bodhisattva leaders, who vow to spread the Lotus Sutra in the Saha world. *"...Among these bodhisattvas, there were four leaders. The first leader was called Superior Actions, the second leader was called Boundless Actions, the third leader was called Pure Actions, and the fourth leader was called Steadfast Actions. These four bodhisattvas were the foremost teachers and leaders among the assembly." (LS 15: 1.8)*

Chapter 16 – Eternal Lifespan of Tathagata	Shakyamuni Buddha reveals his past attainment of Buddhahood since incalculable kalpas ago. He also tells the Parable of a Skillful Doctor to explain how the Buddha applies the expedient method and gives away the best medicine to save people from bitter suffering. *"Thereupon, knowing that the bodhisattvas had requested three times consecutively, the Bhagavat proclaimed: 'O disciples! Listen carefully to the secret divine powers of Tathagata! All heavenly gods, humans, and asuras in the entire Universe believe that the present Shakyamuni Buddha, who left the palace of Shakya not far from the city of Gaya, attained Supreme Perfect Enlightenment at the sanctuary of the Way. O virtuous men! In truth, however, it has been immeasurably boundless hundreds of thousands of millions of billions of nayuta kalpas since I became a Buddha.'"* *(LS 16: 1.3)*
Chapter 17 – Distinctions in Merits	The Buddha bestows prophecy of Buddhahood for those who respond with joy upon hearing the teaching of eternal life of the Buddha (Dharmakaya) in Chapter 16. This is because those who embrace the Lotus Sutra have bountiful virtues and blessings.

	"Having acquired merits upon hearing with joy the eternal lifespan of the Buddha, these virtuous men and women will definitely attain Supreme Perfect Enlightenment." *(LS 17: 2.3)*
Chapter 18 – Merits of Spontaneous Joy in Law	The Buddha teaches that people who receive the teaching of the Lotus Sutra with joy will have immeasurable blessings, and they will be able to widely spread the Dharma of Buddhahood. This shows the importance of happiness in the Dharma practice. *"O Ajita! The blessings received by even the fiftieth person who, in turn, hears the Lotus Sutra and accepts with spontaneous joy are indeed immeasurably boundless asamkhya. How much more so of someone who is the first in the assembly to hear and respond with joy! The good fortune of that person is peerless and unrivaled, beyond the number of immeasurably boundless asamkhya!" (LS 18: 1.9)*
Chapter 19 – Merits of the Teachers of the Law	The Buddha expounds that those who teach others about the Lotus Sutra will result in the spiritual purification of six sense organs. *"...If there are virtuous men and women who accept and embrace the Lotus Sutra by reading, reciting, explaining, expounding, copying, or*

	transcribing it, these people will receive eight hundred merits for the eyes, twelve hundred merits for the ears, eight hundred merits for the nose, twelve hundred merits for the tongue, eight hundred merits for the body, and twelve hundred merits for the mind. These merits serve to adorn, cleanse, and purify their six senses." (*LS 19: 1.1*)
Chapter 20 – Bodhisattva Never Disrespectful	The Buddha shares how, in his past life as Bodhisattva Never Disrespectful—who practiced the virtues of endurance, patience, and perseverance—he was able to receive the teachings of the Lotus Sutra from the King of Majestic Voices Buddha. The Buddha also reiterates that the Lotus Sutra is the main cause for his quick attainment of Buddhahood. *"O Gainer of Great Authority! Who do you think this Bodhisattva Never Disrespectful was at that time? This person is none other than I myself! In my previous lifetime, had I not accepted, embraced, read, recited, and expounded the Lotus Sutra for others, I would never have been able to attain Supreme Perfect Enlightenment so quickly. Because I accepted, embraced, read, recited, and expounded the Lotus Sutra for others in the presence of the former Buddhas, I was able to*

	quickly attain Supreme Perfect Enlightenment. *(LS 20: 1.15)*
Chapter 21 – Divine Powers of Tathagata	The Buddha exhorts his disciples to single-mindedly practice the Lotus Sutra because it is the essence of the Buddha's teachings. *"In essence, I have revealed and expounded all the teachings of Tathagata, all the effortless divine powers of Tathagata, all the Secret Treasuries of Tathagata, and all the profound historical events of Tathagata in the Lotus Sutra. Therefore, after the parinirvana of Tathagata, all of you shall single-mindedly practice the Law by accepting, embracing, reading, reciting, explaining, preaching, copying, and transcribing the Lotus Sutra."* *(LS 21: 1.8)*
Chapter 22 – Entrustment	The Buddha entrusts his disciples to spread the Lotus Sutra—the Dharma of Buddhahood—after his parinirvana. *"...For immeasurable hundreds of thousands of millions of billions of asamkhya kalpas, I have practiced this Law of Supreme Perfect Enlightenment that is rare and difficult to attain. Now, I have entrusted the Law to you. You must*

	wholeheartedly focus on widely propagating the Law so as to bring increased benefits, blessings, and prosperity for all." (LS 22: 1.1)
Chapter 23 – Bodhisattva Medicine King	The Buddha teaches the virtue of generosity in the attainment of Buddhahood through the example of Bodhisattva Medicine King. The bodhisattva practices supreme devotion through offerings to the Buddha. However, the Buddha also expounds that embracing the Lotus Sutra is the most eminent type of offerings to the Buddha that results in the greatest of blessings. *"Furthermore, if there are people who give Three Thousand Major Thousandfold Worlds overflowing with seven treasures as offerings to the Buddhas, great bodhisattvas, pratyekabuddhas, and arhats, their merits gained could not surpass that of someone who accepts and embraces the Lotus Sutra, even if it is only one stanza consisting of four lines in the entire sutra. In other words, the one who embraces the Lotus Sutra has the most blessings." (LS 23: 2.3)*
Chapter 24 – Bodhisattva Wonderful Music	The Buddha teaches the virtue of making the trip to listen to the Dharma and establishing friendship with Dharma friends. Through the example of Bodhisattva Wonderful Music, we also know that performing music is a splendid way of giving offering to the Triple Gem.

	"O Splendid Virtue! Bodhisattva Wonderful Music is able to save and protect various living beings in the Saha world. Bodhisattva Wonderful Music transforms and manifests himself in different forms so as to expound the Lotus Sutra for all living beings in the Saha world. Yet his divine powers, his transformations, and his wisdom will never deteriorate." *(LS 24: 2.8)*
Chapter 25 – Universal Gateway of Bodhisattva Avalokitesvara	Bodhisattva Avalokitesvara is the embodiment of love, grace, and compassion. Just being mindful of this bodhisattva will enable us to develop loving-kindness and compassion. As such, to become a Buddha, we must first practice unconditional love and compassion. *"Have no doubts whatsoever! Always be mindful of the holy and pure Bodhisattva Avalokitesvara. He is the one in whom you can take refuge in the throes of suffering, agony, death, and calamity." (LS 25: 2.23)*
Chapter 26 – Dharani	An alternative way to practice the Lotus Sutra is through providing support and assistance to the practitioners of the Lotus Sutra. Thus, to become a Buddha, protect the Sangha and your Dharma friends.

	"At that moment, Bodhisattva Medicine King said to the Buddha: 'O Bhagavat! I wish to give the dharani to the Teachers of the Law so as to guard and protect them.'" *(LS 26: 1.4)*
Chapter 27 – History of King Magnificent Glory	Through the example of King Magnificent Glory, the Buddha teaches the paramount importance of relationship with Dharma friends in helping one attain Buddhahood. In short, the Dharma friends are Great Causes that enable us to become a Buddha. *"O Great King! You should know that a good friend is the reason—the great cause and condition—that results in one being transformed and being able to meet a Buddha. It is also the reason for the awakening of the desire to attain Supreme Perfect Enlightenment."* *(LS 27: 2.12)*
Chapter 28 – Encouragement of Bodhisattva Universal Worthy	Bodhisattva Universal Worthy is a personification of great vows, actions, and meditation. He is the bodhisattva who ensures widespread propagation of the Lotus Sutra on Earth. As the guardian of the Lotus Sutra, he protects all practitioners of the Lotus Sutra. Therefore, one of the bodhisattva virtue is to make a vow and take concrete actions to translate ideas into reality.

"O Universal Worthy! If there are people who accept, embrace, read, and recite the Lotus Sutra, meditate and memorize it correctly, as well as practice the sutra as it is taught, you should know that these people have already seen Shakyamuni Buddha. It is as though they have heard the Lotus Sutra directly from the mouth of Shakyamuni Buddha. You should know that these people have given offerings to Shakyamuni Buddha. You should know that these people have been praised 'Excellent!' by Shakyamuni Buddha. You should know that these people have been patted on the head by Shakyamuni Buddha. You should know that these people have been covered in the robes of Shakyamuni Buddha."
(LS 28: 2.2)

Appendix 6: Mandalas Used in Nichiren Shu and Soka Gakkai

Members of different Nichiren sects use slightly different styles of the Gohonzon, the object of worship in Nichiren Buddhism. Soka Gakkai uses the Nichikan-transcribed Gohonzon, and Nichiren Shu uses the Shutei Mandala, which is purported to be the closest replica of the Gohonzon inscribed by Nichiren himself. As for Nichiren Shoshu, the current Gohonzon is a transcription by the current 68th High Priest, Nichinyo. Each high priest disseminates his own transcription that reflects the Dai-Gohonzon. However, the most popular Nichiren Shoshu Gohonzon is the Nittatsu Gohonzon.

In the interest of simplicity, we will give you an overview comparison of the content in the Nichiren Gohonzon (Soka Gakkai) and Shutei Mandala (Nichiren Shu).

Nichikan Gohonzon

Nichikan Gohonzon is the Gohonzon issued to the members of the Soka Gakkai worldwide. This Gohonzon is transcribed by the 26th chief priest of Taiseki-ji, the head temple of the Nikko school (Fuji School) which currently belongs to the Nichiren Shoshu sect.

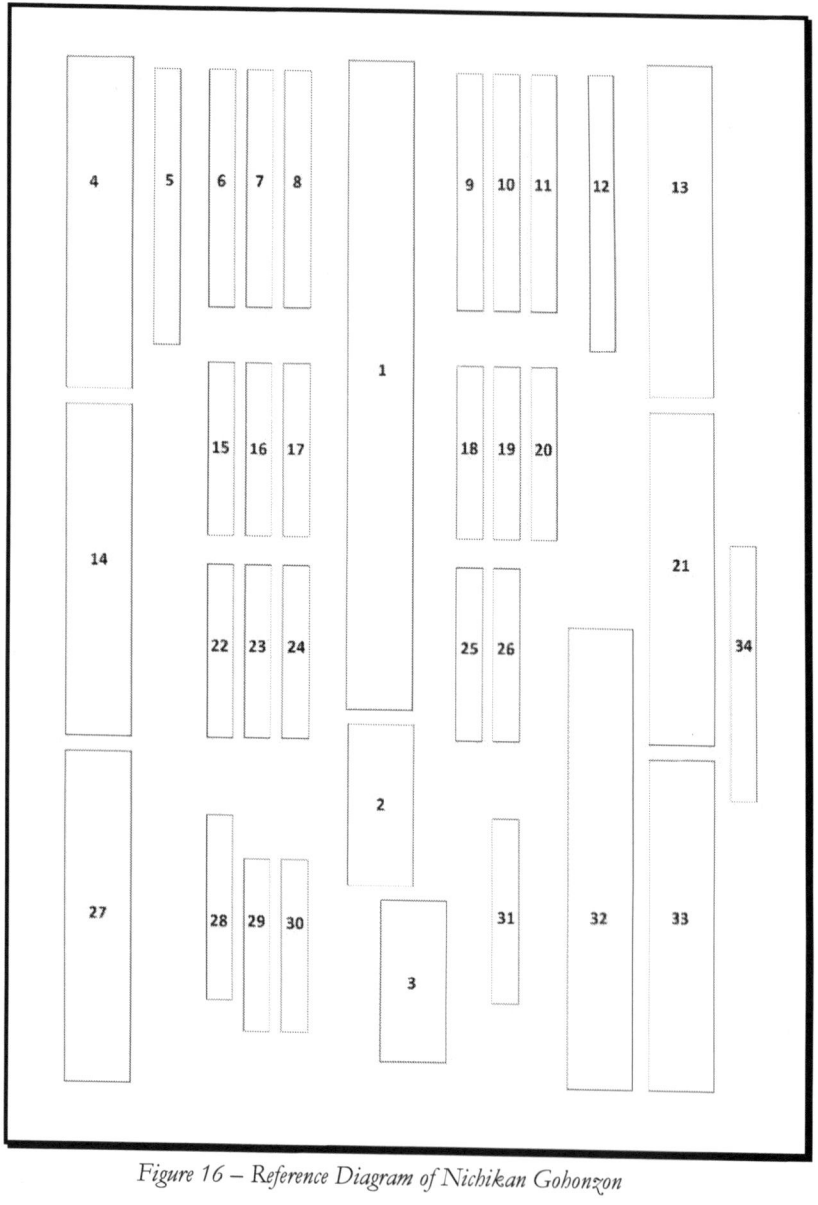

Figure 16 – Reference Diagram of Nichikan Gohonzon

Shutei Mandala

Shutei Mandala[6] is the object of worship used by members of the Nichiren Shu. It is believed that this mandala was the closest replica inscribed by Nichiren Shonin himself.

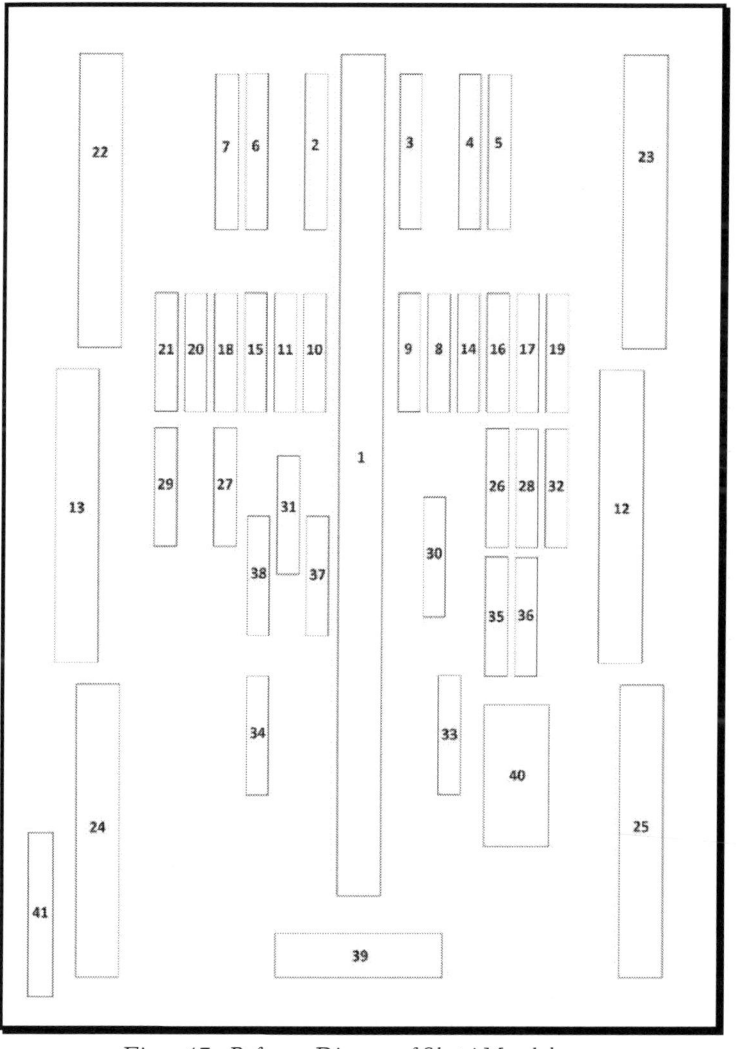

Figure 17 - Reference Diagram of Shutei Mandala

Comparisons between Shutei Mandala (SM) and Nichikan Gohonzon

Ref. No. of SM	Content of Shutei Mandala (SM)	Remarks / Descriptions in Nichikan Gohonzon	Nichikan Gohonzon's Reference Number
1	Namu Myoho Renge Kyo 南无妙法莲华经	The meaning of the seven Chinese characters is "Devotion to the Lotus Sutra of the Magnificent Law"	Yes (1)
2	Shakyamuni Buddha 释迦牟尼佛	Historical Buddha and founder of Buddhism. He is the protagonist of the Lotus Sutra expounding the Dharma of enlightenment from his personal experience of remote past.	Yes (8)
3	Abundant Treasures Tathagata 多宝如来	The ancient Buddha who appeared in Chapter 11 from the pagoda that sprang out of the earth, suspended in mid-air. He vowed to appear anywhere the moment the Lotus Sutra was preached.	Yes (9)

Ref. No. of SM	Content of Shutei Mandala (SM)	Remarks / Descriptions in Nichikan Gohonzon	Nichikan Gohonzon's Reference Number
4	Bodhisattva Superior Actions 上行菩萨	The chief of the four Bodhisattvas of the Earth who appeared in Chapter 15. He is believed to represent the virtue of True Self. Nichiren claims that he is the reincarnation of this bodhisattva.	Yes (10)
5	Bodhisattva Boundless Actions 无边行菩萨	This bodhisattva of the earth is believed to represent the virtue of Eternity.	Yes (11)
6	Bodhisattva Pure Actions 净行菩萨	This bodhisattva of the earth is believed to represent the virtue of Purity.	Yes (7)
7	Bodhisattva Steadfast Actions 安立行菩萨	This bodhisattva of the earth is believed to represent the virtue of Happiness.	Yes (6)
8	Bodhisattva Medicine King 药王菩萨	Bodhisattva Medicine King appears numerous times in Chapters 10, 13, 23, and 26 of the Lotus Sutra. Zhiyi is considered to be a manifestation of this bodhisattva because he claimed to have attained Buddhahood through Chapter 23.	No

Ref. No. of SM	Content of Shutei Mandala (SM)	Remarks / Descriptions in Nichikan Gohonzon	Nichikan Gohonzon's Reference Number
9	Bodhisattva Manjushri 文殊菩萨	Bodhisattva Manjushri is the personification of transcendent wisdom as he is associated with the Perfection of Wisdom Sutras. He appears in Chapters 1, 12, 14, and 24 of the Lotus Sutra.	No
10	Bodhisattva Universal Worthy 普贤菩萨	Bodhisattva Universal Worthy is the embodiment of vow and actions. He appears in Chapter 28 of the Lotus Sutra as well as the closing sutra—The Sutra of Meditation on Bodhisattva Universal Worthy.	No
11	Bodhisattva Maitreya 弥勒菩萨	Bodhisattva Maitreya is the future Buddha after Shakyamuni Buddha. He appears numerous times in the Lotus Sutra: Chapters 1, 15, 16, 17, 18.	No

Ref. No. of SM	Content of Shutei Mandala (SM)	Remarks / Descriptions in Nichikan Gohonzon	Nichikan Gohonzon's Reference Number
12	Immovable Lord Knowledge King (Skt. Acalanatha Vidyaraja, Jp. Fudo Myo-o) 不动明王	A wrathful deity and the Dharma protector in esoteric, Tendai, and Vajrayana Buddhism. He is very popular in Japan as a destroyer of all types of evil: demons, black magic, and sickness. Note: He does not appear in the Lotus Sutra.	Yes (21)
13	Desire King Knowledge King (Skt. Ragaraja Vidyaraja, Jp. Aizen Myo-o) 愛染明王	A wrathful deity and the Dharma protector in esoteric, Tendai, and Vajrayana Buddhism. He is very popular among geisha, artisans, and those who are concerned with love and sensual desire in Japan. Note: He does not appear in the Lotus Sutra.	Yes (14)
14	Shariputra 舍利弗	The Buddha's disciple who is the personification of wisdom. He appears in Chapters 2 and 3 of the Lotus Sutra.	No

Ref. No. of SM	Content of Shutei Mandala (SM)	Remarks / Descriptions in Nichikan Gohonzon	Nichikan Gohonzon's Reference Number
15	Mahakashyapa 摩诃迦叶	The Buddha's disciple who is the personification of ascetic practices. He appears in Chapters 3, 4 and 6 of the Lotus Sutra.	No
16	Great Brahma Heavenly King 大梵天王	Great Brahma is known as the Lord of the Saha World in Chapter 1 and 23. He is the creator of the world of form. He appears in Chapters 1, 2, 18, 19, 24, and 25 of the Lotus Sutra.	Yes (18)
17	King Mara of the Sixth Heaven 第六天魔王	Mara means "murderer." King Mara lives in the highest heaven in the realm of desire. He can manipulate and exploit other beings in the realm of desire, including deities in lower heavenly realms. He appears in Chapters 2 and 12 of the Lotus Sutra.	Yes (19)

Ref. No. of SM	Content of Shutei Mandala (SM)	Remarks / Descriptions in Nichikan Gohonzon	Nichikan Gohonzon's Reference Number
18	Shakra Devanam Indra 帝釈天王	Shakra is the almighty lord of the 33 deities in the Heaven of the Thirty-three Gods at the summit of Mount Sumeru. Also known as Vajrapani, he is the commander-in-chief of the four heavenly kings. He appears in Chapters 1, 2, 18, 19, 24, and 25 of the Lotus Sutra.	Yes (17)
19	Surya 大日天王	Surya is the Indian Vedic God of the Sun, known as one of the 33 gods in the Heaven of the Thirty-Three Gods. In esoteric Buddhism, he represents bodhicitta. His name does not appear in the Lotus Sutra.	Yes (20)
20	Chandra 大月天王	Chandra is the Indian Vedic God of the Moon, known as one of the 33 gods in the Heaven of the Thirty-Three Gods. In esoteric Buddhism, he represents the Buddha-nature that purifies that three poisons.	Yes (16)

Ref. No. of SM	Content of Shutei Mandala (SM)	Remarks / Descriptions in Nichikan Gohonzon	Nichikan Gohonzon's Reference Number
		His name does not appear in the Lotus Sutra.	
21	Aruna Myojo Tunji 大明星天王	He is Indian Vedic God of the Star that is associated with Venus, the morning star. His name does not appear in the Lotus Sutra.	Yes (15)
22	Heavenly King of the North (Skt. Vaishravana, Jp. Dai Bishamon Tunno) 大毗沙門天王	Chief of the Four Heavenly Kings, the Guardian King of the North. His name means 'He who is knowing,' or 'He who hears everything in the kingdom.' Servingunder Indra, he is black in color, thus known as the 'black warrior.' Presiding over winter, his symbols are a jewel and a serpent. He commands a large army of Yaksas. In Chapter 26, he offers a Dharani to protect practitioners of the Lotus Sutra.	Yes (4)

Ref. No. of SM	Content of Shutei Mandala (SM)	Remarks / Descriptions in Nichikan Gohonzon	Nichikan Gohonzon's Reference Number
		Note: While the specific names of the four heavenly kings are not mentioned, their presence is found in the Lotus Sutra.	
23	Heavenly King of the East (Skt. Dhritarashtra, Jp. Dai Jilcolcu Tunno) 大持国天王	Presiding over spring, he is the Guardian King of the East. His name means 'He who maintains the kingdom (of the Law),' or 'the maintainer of the state.' He is the commander of the heavenly musicians known as the Gandharvas, as well as vampires, demons, and hungry ghosts known as the Pishacha.	Yes (13)
24	Heavenly King of the South (Skt. Virudhaka, Dai Zocho Tunno) 大増长天王	Presiding over summer, he is the Guardian King of the South. His name means 'He who enlarges the kingdom,' or 'the powerful one.' His army consists of the kumbhandas (spirit-eating demons known for their human bodies, horse heads, and huge scrotums) and the pretas (hungry ghosts).	Yes (27)

Ref. No. of SM	Content of Shutei Mandala (SM)	Remarks / Descriptions in Nichikan Gohonzon	Nichikan Gohonzon's Reference Number
		In Chapter 26, he offers a Dharani to protect practitioners of the Lotus Sutra.	
25	Heavenly King of the West (Skt. Virupaksha, Jp. Dai Komoku Tunno) 摩诃迦叶	Presiding over autumn, he is the Guardian King of the West. His name means 'He who observes everything that happens in the king-dom,' or 'He who sees all.' His army consists of nagas (dragons or serpents of the oceans/rivers) and putanas (hungry ghosts who are associated with fevers and with the protection of pregnant women).	Yes (33)
26	Wheel Turning Kings (Skt. Chakravartin, Jp. Tunrin Jo-o) 转轮圣王	They are virtuous and powerful monarchs who rule with justice rather than violence in the realm of humans. King Ashoka, who supports the propagation of Buddhism, is known to be a Wheel Turning King.	No

Ref. No. of SM	Content of Shutei Mandala (SM)	Remarks / Descriptions in Nichikan Gohonzon	Nichikan Gohonzon's Reference Number
27	King Ajatashatru 阿闍世王	King of Magadha who was influenced by Devadatta to kill his father, King Bimbisara. He subsequently repented his mistakes and took refuge in the Triple Gem. His name appears in Chapter 1 of the Lotus Sutra.	No
28	Asura Kings 阿修罗王	One of the eight kinds of supernatural beings known to protect the Dharma. Characterized by envy, pride, jealousy, and ego, they are always fighting against devas. Asura kings appear in Chapter 1 of the Lotus Sutra.	No
29	Dragon Kings (Skt. Naga-rajas) 龙王	One of the eight kinds of supernatural beings known to protect the Dharma. They are the dragons or serpents dwelling beneath the ocean or the rivers. They appear in Chapter 1 of the Lotus Sutra. Dragon King Sagara has a daughter (Chapter 12) who attains Buddhahood through the Lotus Sutra.	Yes (22)

Ref. No. of SM	Content of Shutei Mandala (SM)	Remarks / Descriptions in Nichikan Gohonzon	Nichikan Gohonzon's Reference Number
30	Hariti Kishimojin 鬼子母	A female yaksha (fresh-eating demon/spirit) whose name means "stealer of children." She, together with her 10 daughters, appears in Chapter 26 to offer dharani and protection to the teacher of the Lotus Sutra.	Yes (25)
31	Ten Female Rakshasas (Jp. Jurasetsunyo) 十罗刹女	Daughters of Hariti who offer Dharani and vow to protect the teacher of the Lotus Sutra in Chapter 26. They appear as beautiful women wielding weapons or symbolic objects.	Yes (24)
32	Devadatta 提婆达多	Devadatta was the Buddha's first cousin and Ananda's brother. Ambitious and jealous of the Buddha, he attempted to kill the Buddha several times but to no avail. In Chapter 12 of the Lotus Sutra, he was a good friend who taught the Buddha the Lotus Sutra in the Buddha's past life. He is predicted to become a	No

Ref. No. of SM	Content of Shutei Mandala (SM)	Remarks / Descriptions in Nichikan Gohonzon	Nichikan Gohonzon's Reference Number
		Buddha named Heavenly King	
33	Tensho Daijin Amaterasu Omikami 天照大神	A Shinto sun goddess.	Yes (31)
34	Hachiman Daibosatsu 八幡大菩薩	A Shinto God of War. The term "Hachiman" means "Eight Banners."	Yes (28)
35	Bodhisattva Nagarjuna 龙树菩萨	Having written numerous commentaries related to the philosophy of Emptiness and the Middle Way, he is the founder of Madhyamaka school of Buddhism. He is also considered as honorary first patriarch of the Tiantai school.	No
36	Zhiyi 智顗大师	The fourth patriarch of Tiantai lineage, he is generally considered as founder of Tiantai Buddhism in China.	Yes (26)
37	Zhanran/Chan-jan, Master Miao-lo	The sixth partriarch of Tiantai Buddhism who revitalized Tiantai school by refuting the claims of	No

Ref. No. of SM	Content of Shutei Mandala (SM)	Remarks / Descriptions in Nichikan Gohonzon	Nichikan Gohonzon's Reference Number
	湛然，妙乐大师	rival schools. He wrote commentaries on the three major works of Zhiyi: Annotations on the Words and Phrases of the Lotus Sutra, Commentary on the Profound Meaning of the Lotus Sutra, and Annotations on the Great Concentration and Insight.	
38	Saicho, Great Master Dengyo 最澄，伝教大师	Founder of Tendai Buddhism in Japan.	Yes (23)
39	Nichiren 日莲	Founder of Nichiren Buddhism. The Shutei Mandala was inscribed in March of 1280. This was the mandala that Nichiren chanted before he passed away on October 13, 1282.	Yes (2)
40	This Great Mandala was for the first time revealed in the Jambudvipa 2,220 years after the extinction of the Buddha		No

Ref. No. of SM	Content of Shutei Mandala (SM)	Remarks / Descriptions in Nichikan Gohonzon	Nichikan Gohonzon's Reference Number
	3rd month, 3rd year of Koan (1280)		
		Nichiren's personal seal or signature	3
		Those who make offerings will gain good fortune surpassing the ten honorable titles [of the Buddha].	5
		Those who vex and trouble [the practitioner of the Law] will have their heads split into seven pieces. (This statement can be traced to Chapter 26 of the Lotus Sutra.)	12
		I respectfully transcribed this	29
		Never in 2,230 some years since the passing of the Buddha has this great mandala appeared in the world.	32
		The 13th day of the sixth month in the fifth year of Kyoho [1720], cyclical sign kanoe-ne	34
		Nichikan's personal seal	30

Appendix 7: Seven Parables of the Lotus Sutra

#1 - Parable of a Blazing House (Chapter 3)

This parable tells how a wealthy man saved his children from a burning house by telling them about the three fascinating toys—goat carriage, deer carriage, and ox carriage—outside the house that were available for them to grab. Upon hearing about the toys, the children escaped the burning house, and the wealthy man gave them the great white ox carriage as the ultimate supreme gift.

Wisdom of the Parable:

This parable is significant because it tells us how the Buddha guides his disciples of varying capacities and inclinations toward enlightenment by using the expedient tools. This means that whatever we learn in the Early Buddhism of the Theravada traditions, as well as those in the early Mahayana traditions, all belong to the skillful means employed by the Buddha to lead us through the gate of Dharma. The ultimate crown jewel of the Buddha is the Law of Anuttara Samyak Sambodhi (Dharma of One Buddha-Vehicle) revealed in the Lotus Sutra.

The wealthy man is the Buddha who rescues his children from the burning house of the Threefold World by giving them three attractive toys:

- The goat carriage represents the teaching of Four Noble Truths expounded for shravakas (or voice-hearers);
- The deer carriage represents the teaching of Twelve-linked Chains of Causation expounded for pratyekabuddhas (or cause-awakened ones);
- The ox carriage represents the teaching of Six Paramitas expounded for bodhisattvas.

Finally, the white ox carriage is the teaching One Buddha-Vehicle, the Dharma of Supreme Perfect Enlightenment, revealed in

Chapter 2 of the Lotus Sutra for all who wish to receive the secret jewel of the Buddha to attain Buddhahood directly and quickly.

#2 - Parable of the Father and His Lost Son (Chapter 4)

Unlike the previous parable, this parable is told by Mahakashyapa. The parable goes as follows: A boy left his father and wandered around aimlessly until, one day, he stumbled upon a mansion owned by his father. His father recognized his son immediately, and he sent his men to invite his son of low self-esteem to work as a cleaner in his mansion. Years later, his son developed confidence and dignity and was promoted by his father to be a steward of his father's treasury house. The father, before his passing, revealed the truth that the boy was indeed his lost son and he bequeathed all his treasures and inheritances to his son.

Wisdom of the Parable:

Most living beings have inferior aspirations and, as such, they do not believe that they, too, have the capacities to become a Buddha. Therefore, these beings are like the lost son with low self-esteem and low self-confidence. The wealthy father is the Buddha who takes his time to develop confidence and capacity of his son. When the time is right and his son is ready, the father finally reveals the father-and-son relationship between them and bequeaths all his treasures to his son.

The significance of this parable lies in the fact that, while all of us are endowed with the Buddha-nature (the potential to become a Buddha), we need to receive the seed of Buddhahood directly from the Buddha to attain Buddhahood. In other words, there is a lineage of Buddha passing down the baton of Supreme Perfect Enlightenment to his disciples in the form of a "Buddha's inheritance" (i.e. One Buddha-Vehicle). Simply put, the One Buddha-Vehicle in the Lotus Sutra is the precious inheritance given to all who accept and practice the Lotus Sutra as it is taught.

#3 - Parable of the Medicinal Herbs (Chapter 5)

The setting of this parable is Nature and the Kingdom of Plants. While all the six of the seven parables focus on understanding the Buddha as a teacher and father, this is the only parable that focuses on the natures of the Buddha's disciples. The great cloud in the sky gave out rain and moisture equally to various types of trees and plants. There were the three kinds of medicinal herbs (superior, mediocre, or inferior) and two kinds of trees (large or small). All of them thrived abundantly according to their distinctive natures and characteristics as herbs, plants, and trees.

Wisdom of the Parable:

The parable leads us to understand that the Buddha delivers his teachings fairly, but his disciples are different in terms of natures, inclinations, and capacities to understand the Dharma which, in turn, influences the achievement of his disciples. The great cloud is the Buddha, and the various plants are the living beings. The cloud gives out rain equally to all, but each individual plant grows differently. Let us understand the meaning of three kinds of medicinal herbs:

- Inferior herb denotes teachings by heavenly and human beings (including those of Brahma's);
- Mediocre herb denotes teachings for shravakas (Four Noble Truths) and pratyekabuddha (Twelve-linked Chains of Causations);
- Superior herb denotes the Mahayana teaching for Bodhisattva (Six Paramitas);
- The superior herbs are further categorized into two kinds of trees: large and small. The small tree represents individual practice towards Buddhahood while the large tree represents those who lead innumerable people to Buddhahood.

4 - Parable of the Imaginary City (Chapter 7)

This parable shows us the power and leadership of the Buddha in guiding his disciples toward enlightenment. In this parable, the Buddha is a wise and experienced caravan leader who led a group of travellers in search of great treasure. As the journey was long and hazardous, the group became weary, and they wanted to give up half-way and turn back. Therefore, the caravan leader conjured up an imaginary city through his divine powers so that his group could take a rest. Once the group was well-rested, the city was made to vanish, and the caravan leader told them that the city was merely an illusion for them to take a break, and he urged them to continue their journey toward the treasured destination that was close at hand.

Wisdom of the Parable:

A leader needs ingenuity and empathy to spur his people to greatness. The Buddha as the caravan leader knows that some of his disciples need to take a break in the journey of attaining Buddhahood. Thus, the Buddha creates a temporary refuge—a type of imaginary city—by teaching the doctrine of Nibbana and Four Stages of Enlightenment[7] for his disciples to take a respite. This shows that the ultimate goal of Buddhism is not just becoming an arhat, but a completely awakened Buddha.

5 - Parable of the Jewel in the Robe (Chapter 8)

This is a parable about friendship and gifts. The Buddha is a dear friend who bestows the gift of Buddhahood. Here goes the parable: A poor man visited a good friend, but he was soon drunk and fell asleep. His good friend left a priceless jewel by sewing it into the lining of the poor man's robe before going on a business trip. The poor man woke up, not knowing of the jewel in his robe, and resumed his destitute life as a vagrant. One day, he bumped into his good friend who told him of the jewel in the robe. Rejoicing, the poor friend was liberated from abject poverty.

Wisdom of the Parable:

In both Theravada and Mahayana traditions, the Buddha stresses the importance of having a "good friend," the friend of Dharma, who guides us toward enlightenment. Sometimes, the critical seed to enlightenment is whether or not we have any good friends of Dharma in our lives. They can be our parents, grandparents, relatives, colleagues, schoolmates, bosses, spouse or children—they could be any relation to us, so long as they guide us in the practice of Dharma of Buddhahood.

One point to note is that the jewel in the robe is not the Buddha-nature; it is the teaching of One Buddha-Vehicle which enables all to attain enlightenment quickly. Just like a fertile ground, the Buddha-nature is a state of potentiality. The teaching of One Buddha-Vehicle is the Buddha-seed which needs to be planted in the fertile land in order to the Bodhi tree to sprout and grow. Thus, the Dharma is not something naturally endowed; it is a gift given by the Buddha. Whoever practices the Dharma has the gift, and this gift can be shared with others through friendship or kinship.

6 - Parable of the Precious Pearl in the Topknot (Chapter 14)

This parable shows that the Dharma of One Buddha-Vehicle is the ultimate gift for the Seekers of the Law. Once, there was a Holy King of Wheel Turning who rewarded his victorious soldiers by doling out a plethora of lavish gifts such as mansions, clothing, and various treasures of gold and silver. Nonetheless, he kept the only precious pearl in his topknot to himself. This precious pearl was given away only when an outstanding soldier had proven himself worthy by consistently triumphing against evils.

Wisdom of the Parable:

The Buddha is like the king who teaches all types of Dharma—such as meditation, impermanence, suffering, no-self, etc.—as gifts for his disciples. However, he kept to himself the precious pearl in his topknot (which is a metaphor for the Dharma of Buddhahood) until his disciples were ready to accept it. This means that the Law of Supreme Perfect Enlightenment is the crown jewel that is given away when the timing and conditions are right.

7 - Parable of the Skillful Doctor (Chapter 16)

This is a parable about the Buddha as a doctor who heals the pains of his children by leveraging the power of the expedient means in his teachings. The Buddha is like a doctor whose Dharma teachings are powerful medicines capable of curing the most incurable illnesses in life. Here goes the parable:

A skillful doctor was a father of many children. One day, when he was out of town, his children unwittingly consumed poisons. His deranged children implored their father to heal them. The father immediately concocted the most outstanding medicines. Some took the medicines and were cured. Yet, some refused to take the medicines. Hence, the father resorted to skillful means by traveling to a faraway land, leaving behind the medicines, and sending back a message of his own demise. Devastated, the obstinate children came back to their senses. They took the medicines and were cured. The father returned home when he knew all his children were healed.

Wisdom of the Parable:

This parable tells us the true nature of the Buddha's life: the eternal, adamantine Dharmakaya of the Buddha. Shakyamuni Buddha teaches the true aspect of life from his own personal experience. He attained Buddhahood eons ago, and he has never entered parinirvana. He is always there with us, preaching the Dharma of Buddhahood for the liberation of all living begins.

Summary of the Seven Parables of the Lotus Sutra

Seven Parables	Motif
Parable of a Blazing House	Buddha: Father Dharma: Great White Ox Cart Sangha: Children
Parable of the Father and His Lost Son	Buddha: Father Dharma: Inherited Treasures Sangha: Son
Parable of the Medicine Herbs	Buddha: Cloud Dharma: Rain Sangha: Plants and Herbs
Parable of the Imaginary City	Buddha: Caravan Leader Dharma: Imaginary City and Leadership Sangha: Tribe
Parable of the Jewel in the Robe	Buddha: Rich Friend Dharma: Jewel in the Robe Sangha: Poor Friend
Parable of the Precious Pearl in the Topknot	Buddha: King of Wheel Turning Dharma: Pearl in the Topknot Sangha: Soldiers
Parable of the Skillful Doctor	Buddha: Father and Doctor Dharma: Medicine and Method Sangha: Children

Table 10: Summary of the Seven Parables of the Lotus Sutra

Notes

Introduction

1   Longer Sukhāvatīvyūha Sūtra (Infinite Life Sutra), the Shorter Sukhāvatīvyūha Sūtra (Amitabha Sutra) and the Amitayurdhyana Sutra (Contemplation Sutra).

2   "The best books on Buddhism recommended by Donald S. Lopez Jr.," accessed Jan 24, 2018, **https://fivebooks.com/best-books/donald-s-lopez-jr-on-buddhism/**

3   "Is Lotus Sutra authentic?", Sujato's Blog, last accessed March 9, 2018, **https://sujato.wordpress.com/2011/10/18/is-the-lotus-sutra-authentic/**

4   "Rare Lotus Sutra Opens to Public," *Times of India*, last accessed March 9, 2018, **https://timesofindia.indiatimes.com/india/Rare-Lotus-Sutra-opens-to-public/articleshow/12974156.cms**

5   *The Mahayana Mahaparinirvana Sutra,* trans. Kosho Yamamoto (London: Nirvana Publications, 2000)

6   In Maha Parinirvana Sutra, the Buddha teaches that Nirvana is different from Great Nirvana, which is Buddhahood.

7   "Heart Sutra," Terebess Online, last accessed Feb 8, 2018, **https://terebess.hu**

8   "Diamond Sutra," Reluctant Messenger, last accessed Feb 8, 2018, **http://reluctant-messenger.com/diamond_sutra.htm**, Section 31.

9   "Amitabha Sutra," Fo Guang Shan Translation Team, last accessed Feb 8, 2018, **http://ntireader.org/corpus_entry.php?uri=gloss/amitabha-sutra-kumarajiva-gloss.html&html=true**

10   Burton Watson, *The Vimalakirti* (Sutra Columbia University Press; New Ed edition, 2000), Chapter 2, p 36.

11   "Saṃyukta Āgama 379. Turning the Dharma Wheel," translated from Taishō Tripiṭaka volume 2, number 99, last accessed Feb 8, 2018, **https://lapislazulitexts.com/tripitaka/T0099-LL-0379-dharma-wheel**

12 Minerva T.Y. Lee, *The Lotus Sutra and Its Opening and Closing Sutras: A Beautiful Translation with Deep Love from a Lay Buddhist Practitioner* (United States: Amazon Publishing, 2015), 272.

13 Hisao Inagaki，*Sutra on the Buddha of Infinite Life Delivered by Śākyamuni Buddha* (Numata Center for Buddhist Translation and Research, 2003), 58.

14 The womb-born, egg-born, moisture-born, and transformation- born come about in response: the egg-born come from thought, the womb-born are due to emotion, the moisture-born arise from union, and transformations occur through separation. (Shurangama Sutra, Volume 4, Chapter 1. Last accessed 9 April 18, **http://www.cttbusa.org/shurangama4/shurangama4_3 .asp**).

Section 1: *Insights of the Lotus Sutra*

1   Kim Young-Ho, *Tao-sheng's Commentary on the Lotus Sutra* (Albany: State University of New York Press, 1990).

2   Yoshiro Tamura, *Introduction to the Lotus Sutra.* (Boston: Wisdom Publications, 2014), 111.

3   Gudo Wafu Nishijima and Chodo Cross, trans. *Master Dogen's Shobogenzo, Book 1* (Woods Hole, Mass.: Windbell Publications, 1994), 293-321.

4   George Joji Tanabe and Willa Jane Tanabe, *The Lotus Sutra in Japanese Culture* (University of Hawaii Press, 1989), 31.

5   *SSA Buddhist Study Examination Elementary Level Study Material 2016* (Singapore Soka Association, 2016), 17

6   Thich Nhat Hanh, *Peaceful Action, Open Heart: Lessons from the Lotus Sutra* (Parallax Press, 2005).

7   Lee, *The Lotus Sutra*, 112.

8   Ibid., 108-109.

9   "The Seven Factors of Enlightenment," by Piyadassi Thera. Access to Insight, last accessed Feb 9, 2018, **https://www.accesstoinsight.org/lib/authors/piyadassi/wheel001.html**

10 *The Mahayana Mahaparinirvana Sutra,* trans. Kosho Yamamoto (London: Nirvana Publications, 2000), 25.

11 John Snelling, *The Buddhist Handbook: A Complete Guide to Buddhist Teaching and Practice* (London: Century Paperbacks, 1987), 126.

12 Digha Nikaya III.84, Maurice Walshe, *The Long Discourses of the Buddha,* (Boston, MA: Wisdom Publications, 1995), 409.

13 George D. Chryssides, *Historical dictionary of new religious movements* (2nd ed.) (Lanham, Md.: Rowman & Littlefield, 2012) 251.

14 John McRae, *The Sutra of Queen Śrīmālā of the Lion's Roar and the Vimalakīrti Sutra* (Berkeley, CA: Numata Center for Buddhist Translation and Research, 2004), 102.

15   "Expedient Means and 'Lifespan' Chapters," *The Writings of Nichiren Daishonin I*, last accessed Feb 2, 2018, **https://www.nichirenlibrary.org/en/wnd-1/Content/9**

16   "Chapter 2: On Cunda," *Mahaparinirvana Sutra*, last accessed Feb 2, 2018, **http://www.nirvanasutra.net/nirvanasutraa3.htm**

17   Lee, *The Lotus Sutra*, 353.

18   Yamamoto, *Mahayana Mahaparinirvana Sutra*, 36.

19   "Chapter 2: On Cunda," Mahaparinirvana Sutra, last accessed Feb 2, 2018, **http://www.nirvanasutra.net/nirvanasutraa3.htm**

20   Cock's Foot Mountain (Kukkuṭapāda).

21   "Buddha Pronounces the Sūtra of Maitreya Bodhisattva's Attainment of Buddhahood," Buddha Sutras Mantras Sanskrit, last accessed Jan 29, 2018, **http://www.sutrasmantras.info/sutra11.html**

22   "Jataka Tales and Bodily Sacrifice," Representation of Buddhism in Literature., last accessed Mar 1, 2018, **https://buddhistlitds.wordpress.com/portfolio/jataka-tales/**

23   Lee, *The Lotus Sutra*, 430.

Section 2: The Three Ultimate Truths

1   David J. Kalupahana, *The Principles of Buddhist Psychology*, (Delhi: Satguru Publications, 1992), 120.

2   Vigrahavyaavartanii. Bhattacharya, K. *The Dialectical Method of Naagaarjuna*. (Delhi: Motilal Banarsidass 1990 (3rd. ed.)), 70.

3   David Burton, "Is Madhyamaka Buddhism really the middle way? Emptiness and the problem of nihilism," Taylor & Francis Online, last accessed Feb 4, 2018, **http://www.tandfonline.com/doi/abs/10.1080/14639940108573749)**

4   "Tientai Sect III", Buddhistdoor, last accessed 28 Feb 18, **https://web.archive.org/web/20080423124613/http://www.buddhistdoor.com:80/OldWeb/bdoor/archive/nutshell/teach71.htm**

5   Lama Thubten Yeshe, *The Essence of Tibetan Buddhism* (Boston: Lama Yeshe Wisdom Archive, 2001).

6   *The Dhammapada*, trans. F. Max Müller (Kessinger Publishing, 2007), Verse 1.

7   Asai Endō, *The Lotus Sutra as the Core of Japanese Buddhism: Shifts in Representations of its Fundamental Principle*. (Japanese Journal of Religious Studies 41 (1): 2014), 59.

8   Nikkyo, Niwano, (1976), *Buddhism For Today: A Modern Interpretation of the Threefold Lotus Sutra*. (Tokyo: Kosei Publishing Co.,1976), 109.

9   Tamura, *Introduction to the Lotus Sutra,* 117.

10   Lee, *The Lotus Sutra*, 100.

11   Ibid., 107.

12   Paul Groner and Jacqueline I. Stone, "Editors' Introduction: The 'Lotus Sutra' in Japan," *Japanese Journal of Religious Studies* 41, vol. 1 (2014), 7.

13   U. Wogihara and C. Tsuchida, *Saddharmapundarika-sūtram: Romanized and Revised Text of the Bibliotheca Buddhica Publication* (Tokyo: The Sankibo Buddhist Book Store, 1934), 20.

14   The Six Lower Realms are explained in detail in "Thirty-One Planes of Existence" in the Pali Canon. The Four Higher Noble Realms (Shravaka, Pratyekabuddha, Bodhisattva, Buddhahood) are implied in the Lotus Sutra and other Mahayana sutras. They also appear in the commentaries or abhidharma of the Mahayana traditions.

15   "Three Realms of Existence," Nichiren Library, last accessed May 3, 2018, **https://www.nichirenlibrary.org/en/dic/Content/T/165**

16   Bhikkhu Ñāṇamoli, Bhikkhu Bodhi, *The Middle Length Discourses of the Buddha: A Translation of the Majjhima Nikāya* (Wisdom Publication, 1995), 1085.

17   Bhikkhu Bodhi, *The Connected Discourses of the Buddha: A New Translation of the Samyutta Nikaya* (Wisdom Publication, 2000), 1350.

18   Bhikkhu Bodhi, Nyanaponika Thera, *Numerical Discourses of the Buddha: An Anthology of Suttas from the Anguttara Nikaya* (Altamira Press, 2000), 372-373.

19   Lee, *The Lotus Sutra*, 229.

20   Taitetsu Unno, *Shin Buddhism: Bits of Rubble Turn into Gold* (New York: Doubleday, 2002), 35.

21   "Hongaku – Original Enlightenment," Tendai Buddhism UK, last accessed 28 Feb 2018, **https://tendaiuk.com/2015/02/23/hongaku/**

22   John R. McRae, *The Platform Sutra of the Sixth Patriarch* (Numata Center for Buddhist Translation and Research, 2000).

23   John Wong CW, *Awaken Your Healing Power: A Molecular Biologist's Journey in Reversing Paralysis and Blindness through Transcendental Connection* (Candid Creation Publishing, 2011).

Section 3: The Practice of the Lotus Sutra

1   "Tao-sheng," Soka Gakkai, Nichiren Buddhism Library, accessed 23 June 2017, **http://www.nichirenlibrary.org/en/dic/Content/T/18**

2   Young-Ho Kim, "Tao-Sheng's Commentary on the Saddharmapudarika Sutra: A Study and Translation" (PhD Diss., McMaster University, 1985), 25

3   "Amitabha Buddha," last accessed Jan 24, 2018, https://tendaiuk.com/2016/04/18/amitabha-buddha/

4   Ibid.

5   "All Chapters are Nam Myoho Renge Kyo," The Record of the Orally Transmitted Teachings, last accessed Jan 24, 2018, **https://www.nichirenlibrary.org/en/ott/Separate-Transmission/2**

6   Jan Nattier, *The Indian Roots of Pure Land Buddhism: Insights from the Oldest Chinese Versions of the Larger Sukhavativyuha* (Indiana University), 184.

7   "10 Misconceptions about Buddhism: The Primary Form of Buddhist Meditation is Mindfulness," by Robert E. Buswell, Jr. and Donald S. Lopez, Jr., *Tricycle*, last accessed Feb 12, 2018, **https://tricycle.org/magazine/10-misconceptions-about-buddhism/**

8   "Dhammapada Verse 354, Sakkapanha Vatthuh," *Tipitaka Network,* last accessed April 10, 2018, **http://www.tipitaka.net/tipitaka/dhp/verseload.php?verse=354**

9   "观世音菩萨，不可思议之神力，已于过去无量劫中，已作佛竟，号正法明如来，大慈愿力，安乐众生故，现作菩萨。"

10 "观世音菩萨在我前成佛，名正法明如来，我为苦行弟子，十方如来，皆此观自在教化故"

11 "无量寿佛，住立空中。观世音、大势至，是二大士，侍立左右。"

12 "阿弥陀佛正法灭后，过中夜分明相出时，观世音菩萨，于七宝菩提树下，结加趺坐，成等正觉，号普光功德山王如来"

13 Mujū Ichien, Robert E. Morrell, *Sand and Pebbles: The Tales of Muju Ichien, A Voice for Pluralism in Kamakura Buddhism* (SUNY Press, 1985), 142.

Section 4: Vision of the Lotus Sangha

1   "Sexual assaults and violent rages... Inside the dark world of Buddhist teacher Sogyal Rinpoche", *The Telegraph,* last accessed April 11, 2018, **https://www.telegraph.co.uk/men/thinking-man/sexual-assaults-violent-rages-inside-dark-world-buddhist-teacher/**

2   Stephen M. Cherry, Helen Rose Ebaugh, *Global Religious Movements Across Borders: Sacred Service* (New York: Ashgate Publishing, 2014), 84.

3   *The Mahayana Mahaparinirvana Sutra,* trans. Kosho Yamamoto (London: Nirvana Publications, 2000), 73.

4   "Four Universal Vows," *Nichiren Buddhism Library,* last accessed April 20, 2018, **https://www.nichirenlibrary.org/en/dic/Content/F/224**

5   Thomas Cleary, *The Flower Ornament Scripture: A Translation of the Avatamsaka Sutra* (Boston: Shambhala Publications, 1993), 315-316.

6   "Human Revolution," *Soka Gakkai International,* last accessed April 11. 2018, **http://www.sgi.org/about-us/buddhist-concepts/human-revolution.html**

7   "Attadiipaa Sutta: An Island to Oneself" (SN 22.43), translated from the Pali by Maurice O'Connell Walshe. *Access to Insight* (BCBS Edition), 30 November 2013, **http://www.accesstoinsight.org/tipitaka/sn/sn22/sn22.043.wlsh.html**

8   "Maha-parinibbana Sutta: Last Days of the Buddha" (DN 16), translated from the Pali by Sister Vajira & Francis Story. Access to Insight (BCBS Edition), last accessed August 3, 2018, **http://www.accesstoinsight.org/tipitaka/dn/dn.16.1-6.vaji.html**.

9   "Compassion as the Source of Happiness," His Holiness The 14th Dalai Lama of Tibet, last accessed July 3, 2018, **https://www.dalailama.com/messages/compassion-and-human-values/compassion-as-the-source-of-happiness**

10   "Music as Medicine: The Impact of Healing Harmonies," *Harvard Medical School,* last accessed Feb 14, 2018, **https://hms.harvard.edu/sites/default/files/assets/Sites/Longwood_Seminars/Longwood%20Seminar%20Music%20Reading%20Pack.pdf**

11   Daisaku Ikeda, *Songs from my Heart* (New York: I.B.Tauris & Co Ltd), 14.

12   "Nichiren Shoshu True Buddhism," Nichiren Shoshu Temple, last accessed Jan 25, 2018, **https://www.nst.org/**

Section 5: *Mandala of the Lotus Sutra*

1   "Shutei Mandala," Lotus World: An Illustrated Guide to the Gohonzon, last accessed August 3, 2018, **http://www.500yojanas.org/lotusworld/**

2   "SGI Denies the Dai-Gohonzon of the High Sanctuary," *Nichiren Shoshu Temple,* last accessed April 11, 2018, **https://www.nst.org/2015/01/12/sgi-denies-dai-gohonzon-high-sanctuary/**

3   "Why No Protection from the Heavenly Gods?" Writings of Nichiren Daishonin-II, p432, last accessed Jan 24, 2018, http://www.nichirenlibrary.org/en/wnd-2/Content/224

4   "On Reprimanding Hachiman," Writings of Nichiren Daishonin-II, p920, last accessed Jan 24, 2018, http://www.nichirenlibrary.org/en/wnd-2/Content/335

5   Appendices 6: Mandala used in Nichiren Shu and Soka Gakkai.

6   Lee, *The Lotus Sutra*, 435.

7   Ibid., 273.

8   Ibid., 450.

9   Ibid., 460.

10   "What are the four? They should be based on Dharma, not the person; on the meaning, not the letter, on Wisdom, not on consciousness; on import-embracing (i.e. Mahayana) sutras, not on non-import embracing sutras." See: Yamamoto, *The Mahayana Mahaparinirvana Sutra.*

11   Lee, *The Lotus Sutra*, 232

12   "The Vows of Bodhisattva Samantabhadra Sutra," Buddhanet, last accessed Feb 14, 2018, **http://www.buddhanet.net/pdf_file/samantabhadra.pdf**

13 "Cakkavatti Sutta: The Wheel-turning Emperor" (DN 26), translated from the Pali by Thanissaro Bhikkhu. Access to Insight (BCBS Edition), 30 November 2013, **http://www.accesstoinsight.org/tipitaka/dn/dn.26.0.than.html**

14 "Superior Practice Bodhisattva," Lotus World: An Illustrated Guide to the Gohonzon, last accessed August 3, 2018,
http://www.500yojanas.org/lotusworld/

15 George D. Chryssides, *Historical Dictionary of New Religious Movements (2nd ed.).* (Lanham, Md.: Rowman & Littlefield, 2012), 251.

16 "Mandala of the Lotus Sutra," Lotus Happiness, last accessed April 28, 2018, **https://www.lotus-happiness.com/mandala/**

Appendices

1 "10 Quotes about Buddhahood in the Lotus Sutra," *Lotus Happiness,* last accessed April 12, 2018, **https://www.lotus-happiness.com/10-quotes-buddhahood-lotus-sutra/**

2 "10 Quotes on the Law of Emptiness in the Lotus Sutra," *Lotus Happiness,* last accessed April 12, 2018, **https://www.lotus-happiness.com/10-quotes-law-emptiness-lotus-sutra/**

3 "20 Quotes about Meditation in the Lotus Sutra," *Lotus Happiness,* last accessed April 12, 2018, **https://www.lotus-happiness.com/20-quotes-meditation-lotus-sutra/**

4 "10 Quotes of Happiness in the Lotus Sutra," *Lotus Happiness,* last accessed April 12, 2018, **https://www.lotus-happiness.com/10-quotes-happiness-lotus-sutra/**

5 Minerva T.Y. Lee, *The Lotus Sutra and Its Opening and Closing Sutras: A Beautiful Translation with Deep Love from a Lay Buddhist Practitioner* (United States: Amazon Publishing, 2015)

6 "Shutei Mandala," *Lotus World: An Illustrated Guide to the Gohonzon,* last accessed August 3, 2018, http://www.500yojanas.org/lotusworld/

7 Four Stages of Enlightenment are stream-winner/stream-enterer (sotapanna), once-returner (sakadagami), non-returner (anāgāmi), and arhat.

Bibliography

The Saddharmapundarika or The Lotus of the True Law. Translated by Jan Hendrik Kern. Sacred Books of the East, vol. 21. Oxford: Clarendon Press, 1884.

The Lotus Sutra and Its Opening and Closing Sutras. Translated by Burton Watson. Soka Gakkai, 2009.

The Lotus Sutra: A Contemporary Translation of a Buddhist Classic. Translated by Gene Reeve. Rissho Kosei-kai, 2008.

The Threefold Lotus Sutra: The Sutra of Innumerable Meanings, The Sutra of the Lotus Flower of the Wonderful Law, and The Sutra of Meditation on the Bodhisattva Universal Virtue. Translated by Bunno Kato, Yoshiro Tamura, and Kojiro Miyasaka. Tokyo: Kosei, 1975.

The Sutra of the Lotus Flower of the Wonderful Law. Translated by Senchu Murano. Tokyo: Nichiren Shu Headquarters, 1974.

Scripture of the Lotus Blossom of the Fine Dharma. Translated by Leon Hurvitz. New York: Columbia University Press, 1976.

The Lotus Sutra: The White Lotus of the Marvelous Law. Translated by Tsugunari Kubo and Akira Yuyama. Tokyo and Berkeley: Bukyo Dendo Kyokai, 1991.

The Wonderful Dharma Lotus Flower Sutra. Buddhist Text Translation Society. 10 volumes. San Francisco: Sino-American Buddhist Association, 1976–82.

Groner, Paul. *Saicho: The Establishment of the Japanese Tendai School.* Berkeley: Asian Humanities Press, 1984.

Ikeda, Daisaku. *The Heart of the Lotus Sutra: Lectures on the "Expedient Means" and "Life Span" Chapters.* World Tribune Press, 2013.

Ikeda, Daisaku. *The Wisdom of the Lotus Sutra.* 6 volumes. World Tribune Press, 2001.

Lee, Minerva T.Y. *The Lotus Sutra and Its Opening and Closing Sutras: A Beautiful Translation with Deep Love from a Lay Buddhist Practitioner.* United States: Amazon Publishing, 2015.

Lopez, Donald. *The Lotus Sutra: A Biography.* United Kingdom: Princeton University Press, 2016.

Montgomery, Daniel B. *Fire in the Lotus: The Dynamic Buddhism of Nichiren.* London: Mandala, 1991.

Nhat Hanh, Thich. *Peaceful Action, Open Heart: Lessons from the Lotus Sutra.* Berkeley: Parallax, 2009.

Niwano, Kosho. *The Buddha in Everyone's Heart: Seeking the World of the Lotus Sutra.* Tokyo: Kosei, 2013.

Niwano, Nikkyo. *A Guide to the Threefold Lotus Sutra.* Tokyo: Kosei Publishing Co., 1989.

Reeves, Gene. *A Buddhist Kaleidoscope Essays on the Lotus Sutra.* Tokyo: Kosei Publishing Co., 2002.

Reeves, Gene. *The Stories of the Lotus Sutra*. Boston: Wisdom Publications, 2010.

Tamura, Yoshiro and Gene Reeves. *Introduction to the Lotus Sutra*. Boston: Wisdom Publications, 2014.

Teiser, Stephen and Jacqueline Stone. *Readings of the Lotus Sutra*. New York: Columbia University Press, 2009.

Stone, Jacqueline I. *Original Enlightenment and the Transformation of Medieval Japanese Buddhism*. Honolulu: University of Hawaii Press, 1999.

Swanson, Paul L. *Foundations of T'ien-T'ai Philosophy: The Flowering of the Two Truths Theory in Chinese Buddhism*. Berkeley: Asian Humanities Press, 1989.

Watson, Burton. *The Essential Lotus: Selections from the Lotus Sutra*. New York: Columbia University Press, 2001.

Yamamoto, Kosho. *The Mahayana Mahaparinirvana Sutra*. London: Nirvana Publications, 2000.

About the Author

Minerva T.Y. Lee has been practicing Nichiren Buddhism since the age of 16. Born in 1983 and raised as a Chinese Buddhist in Malaysia, Minerva learned about the Lotus Sutra from her maternal grandmother who taught her the daimoku of "Nam Myoho Renge Kyo."

The Lotus Sutra is the love of her life. Passionate about the Law of Buddhahood, she shared the joy of Dharma by publishing her first book in 2014, *The Lotus Sutra and Its Opening and Closing Sutras: A Beautiful Translation with Deep Love from a Lay Buddhist Practitioner.*

Minerva is convinced that the most reliable teachers are the Buddhist sutras as well as the Inner Teacher inside us. She advocates self-directed learning of the Buddhist scriptures as the way to learn the Dharma directly from the Buddha. She also believes that empowerment begins by focusing upon one's strengths and natural gifts as a way to unleash one's greatest potentials within.

With a heart full of joy, faith, and gratitude to the Law of Buddhahood, she aspires to be a beacon of hope and change in the practice of the Lotus Sutra for the peace, happiness, and prosperity of humanity.

Currently, Minerva is living with her family in Singapore. She can be reached via:

Website: **http://www.lotus-happiness.com**
Email: **minerva_lotus@yahoo.com**
Facebook: **http://www.facebook.com/LotusHappiness**

43329654R00131

Made in the USA
Lexington, KY
27 June 2019